ST. M̶A̶ ̶ ̶ ̶ ̶ ̶ ̶ ̶ ̶ ̶ AND

W9-ASR-498

UNIVERSITY OF MARYLAND
COLLEGE PARK, MARYLAND

PROBLEMS OF SOCIALISM TODAY

45383

PROBLEMS
OF
SOCIALISM TODAY

by
SANTIAGO CARRILLO
General Secretary of the Communist Party of Spain

1970
LAWRENCE & WISHART
LONDON

Translated by Nan Green and A. M. Elliott
Copyright © Lawrence & Wishart 1970

SBN 85315 222 5

Printed in Great Britain by
Compton Press Compton Chamberlayne Salisbury

CONTENTS

CONTENTS

INTRODUCTION

There have been, and indeed there still are, exiled political
leaders who have remained, as it were, rooted in the situation as it was when they were forced to leave their own
political scene; who fight and re-fight old battles and continue to apply to the changing situation the criteria, the
attitudes, the judgments and justifications of *their* day.
Until, growing older and ever more isolated from their
fellow-countrymen, they become empty figureheads, boring
dummies to the younger generations that have succeeded
them.

That this is not the case with the exiled leaders of the
Spanish Communist Party is shown with singular brilliance
in these selections from the writings of Santiago Carrillo, its
General Secretary. There was a time, it is frankly admitted,
when the number of organised members of their Party was
(understandably, to those who know something of the
Franco terror) greater in the emigration than inside their
own country. But even in those dark days, the concern of
the leadership was not to allow it to become a Party of
emigrés, clearest evidence of which is the long list of leading
members who returned to their country to face imprison-
ment and death for their clandestine work, and the fact that
the several Congresses that have been held since 1939 have
invariably given more representation to delegates from inside
the country than from outside. Today, the situation has
radically changed. Writing in 1967 (the first article in this
collection), Santiago Carrillo states: "We do not need to
ask ourselves what to do to become a mass party; we need

to ask *how we have become a mass party*, in order to find the way to continue our development in this direction."

In 1965, Santiago Carrillo published a book giving his Party's proposals for the future of Spain. Entitled *After Franco, What?*, it examined the situation as it was developing, the widespread struggle of the students, the growing radicalisation of the peasantry, the increasing, and increasingly open, disquiet of the intellectuals, and the powerful growth and fighting spirit of that brilliant invention of the Spanish working class, the "Workers' Commissions", which have completely bypassed the stultifying structures of the state-controlled Vertical Syndicates, the so-called trade unions of the Franco regime. He outlined the plan for democratic development in Spain as envisaged by the Spanish Communists—in the new Spain, the Spain of the 1960s and 1970s.

In 1967, Santiago Carrillo reopened the question of Spain's future in a booklet entitled *A New Look at Present-day Problems*, a major part of which forms the first of the three items here translated. Here again he deals with the new forces, the new alignments, the contemporary problems which the growing forces of democracy are meeting and tackling. It is impossible, reading this hard-hitting, closely-reasoned exposition, to think for a moment that its writer is in any but the closest touch with events, developments and feelings inside Spain. And withal it is a document for discussion, not a set programme but a programme of change for a changing situation; not merely a goal but a way to reach that goal.

The second section of this book consists of a speech made, early in 1968, in preparation for the Spanish Communist Party's participation in the preliminary discussions for the International Conference of Communist and Workers' Parties, which was held the following year. Its range extends to the problems which concern the international movement, as seen from the actual experience of revolutionary struggle in Spain.

Santiago Carrillo grasps nettles firmly. When he sees a problem, however unpleasant it may be, he states it, without pretending to know all the answers, calling for "the ending of paralysing taboos" on full discussion, for "an open-minded, searching attitude, an effort to come to grips with the new factors and new forces" in the world of today. The third article, published in the theoretical quarterly *Nuestra Bandera* in the latter part of 1968, again enters into the debate in the socialist camp and stresses the need to build unity on the basis of *diversity*. "We should certainly not complain about having these problems", he writes, "for they are a consequence of the progress and successes of the world revolution, which has already placed the leadership of fourteen states in the hands of Marxist-Leninist parties. ... When instead of fourteen states we have twenty or thirty, we shall probably have more problems. Instead of lamenting this we should congratulate ourselves that we have them, so long as we do not shut our eyes to the new questions that our own victories pose for us, so long as we foresee them and watch out for their correct solution."

It is with gratitude for the refreshing clarity of this view, and from the wish to share it with others who cannot read Spanish, that we have translated the articles which follow. They cannot help but renew the admiration which so many people in this country feel for the Spanish people's long and heroic struggle for freedom. They cannot help but increase the confidence that the Spanish people will win that struggle.

In a speech made to a group of members of the Spanish Communist Party in April 1969, Santiago Carrillo spoke of a moving letter which had been received by the anti-Franco broadcasting station *Radio España Independiente*. It came from a young correspondent in Valencia who was deeply troubled by the difficulties in the socialist camp. "If the countries that are already socialist cannot overcome these difficulties," he wrote, "what good does it do for us to go to prison, to suffer torture and degrading treatment in Spain, Portugal, Greece and so many other countries struggling against capitalism? . . . We have to struggle not only against Franco but also against the doubts of many of our own friends and comrades, at present."

Santiago Carrillo replied in these words : "I believe that this letter, comrades, expresses in truth the situation, the disquiet and anxiety among many Party members. And I believe too that the broad sections of the youth who sympathise with Communism and would come, and will come, to the Communist Party of Spain, hesitate and feel doubtful when they see these conflicts and problems. And I want to reply from this platform, through *Radio España Independiente*, to this comrade, conscious that many others feel as he does. I want to say to him : yes, comrade, it is worth going to prison, in Spain or in Greece, it is worth giving one's life if necessary for the cause of socialism and freedom. With all its deformations, with all its problems, socialism is the only system which puts an end to capitalist exploitation, it is the only system in which the material and moral conditions can be created for the development of freedom, for the development of man. And the fact that up to now the socialist countries have not attained the perfection of socialism as you have conceived it and as it is conceived by the workers and the youth, does not mean that socialism is not worth striving for. It means that even after winning socialism it is necessary to go on struggling so that socialism may ever become, may ever correspond more closely to the socialism of Marx, Engels and Lenin. And obviously we must struggle. We must struggle against Francoism, we must struggle against capitalism, and we must struggle inside our movement, comrades, to make socialism continually more like socialism . . ." The rest of the sentence was drowned in applause.

NAN GREEN

A NEW LOOK AT PRESENT-DAY PROBLEMS

From *Nuevos Enfoques a Problemas de Hoy,* published in 1967 by Editions Sociales, Paris.

A NEW LOOK AT PRESENT-DAY BIOLOGY

NEW LOOK AT PRESENT-DAY PROBLEMS

For a New Climate in Political and Social Relations

GETTING RID OF THE SECTARIANISM AND STEREOTYPED ATTITUDES OF THE PAST

It may be that the desire to achieve a new climate in social and political relations is now more widespread than it seems to be at first sight. Why get obsessed with the past and why remain chained to it, when so many new phenomena, so many possibilities for the future demand our attention and call for action on our part?

It is certain that if this new climate is to be achieved, then stubborn sectarianism, routine ways of thinking and deep-rooted conditioned reflexes in relation to ideological and political trends will have to be overcome. In order to create this new climate, in order to introduce it into Spanish life, it is necessary to come to terms with everything that has changed, everything that is changing and everything that is inevitably going to change.

It is necessary to adopt an attitude of curiosity, a questing attitude, leaving the well-trodden paths.

It is necessary to jettison "ready-made" ideas, the notion that if things happened in a particular way in the past, it is impossible for them to happen in another way now. It is essential that attitudes should be rejuvenated and brought up to date, to the level of present problems, present needs

15

and present tasks.

We communists are making every effort to bring this about. We consider that the policy of national reconciliation, our new look at the Catholic problem and at the role and autonomy of mass movements; our readiness to engage in a dialogue, even with sections whose convictions are very far removed from our own; the overcoming of any spirit of revenge and our desire to reach a definite degree of national understanding as regards the attainment and preservation of political liberties, demonstrate that we are working sincerely for a new climate in the country's social and political relations. It is in this direction that we are going, in harmony with the state of mind that prevails today among great masses of people, and particularly among the younger generations.

The book *Cartas del pueblo espanol* ("Letters from the Spanish People"), published by Señor Gil Robles and a group of political friends of the former leader of the CEDA*, could represent a positive contribution to this renewal of the political atmosphere. Although it contains very contradictory ideas which detract from the effect of some of the solutions put forward, the book reflects a considerable evolution in some personalities of the Right. Señor Gil Robles and his friends declare themselves to be in favour of democracy, a multi-party system, a constituent assembly, regional autonomy; in favour of a single working-class trade union organisation and an agrarian reform whose "fundamental goal . . . should be that those who cultivate the soil ought to enjoy its fruits." In the book it is stated that, "everything indicates that we are approaching one of the critical periods in our history, when many principles and institutions which our egoism has raised to the category of dogmas, will have to undergo a complete revision." "The alternative," says Señor Robles, "is plain : either a radical transformation by an evolutionary path, or else a violent revolution." The evolution of Gil Robles' positions is

* Confederación Española de Derechas Autónomas, a Spanish

considerable, so much so that if in 1934 the right-wing force which he headed had taken the stand he now upholds, then there would have been no revolutionary movement in October of that year, nor would there have been a fascist rebellion in July 1936; the Republic of 1931 would have been preserved and consolidated. Even though everything that is being said now would have carried much more conviction if it had been preceded by a self-critical look at the past, nevertheless what is heard in *Cartas del pueblo español* brings to political argument a sound that is more in key with the times in which we are living.

A very serious effort should be made by every one of the sections which are playing, or are called upon to play, a role in national development, for there are still many instances of sectarianism and many prejudices to be uprooted in the different fields if it is desired to reach that new climate.

Later on we shall refer to that crude integrist sectarianism which continues to divide Spaniards into "wolves" and "lambs", according to whether they are opposed to, or in favour of, the existing political system.

In other sections, too, however, there are instances of sectarianism, stereotyped prejudices, blinkers which restrict the view. Even though virulent, irrational, reactionary anti-communism had lost a great deal of ground in Spain, its influence still persists in the behaviour of persons who regard themselves as democratic and progressive.

Whether or not the people who go in for it are aware of the fact, this kind of anti-communist sectarianism nowadays turns out to be a pernicious contribution making for the preservation of the political forms resulting from civil war. Moreover, the danger can be more serious for the future development of Spain along democratic and peaceful lines.

That type of anti-communism exists, for instance, among some of the leaders of the Spanish Socialist Party who are living in exile, nullifying many of their activities and actually

Catholic party, founded after the fall of the monarchy.

holding back the growth of their party like a leaden weight.

Undoubtedly there have been mistakes and shortcomings on our side—and on theirs—in our relations in the past. It may be that a retrospective, critical and self-critical examination, on one side and the other, could have a certain value. On condition that its aim was to clear the ground so as to create a new atmosphere of understanding and collaboration. But that critical and self-critical examination of the past, projected towards the future, could on no account be the kind of arbitrary and one-sided indictment frequently levelled against us in the publications and speeches of Socialist Party leaders living in exile—an indictment to which we reply, generally speaking, with silence, so as not to poison the atmosphere still more; an indictment, moreover, which no one can take seriously and from which those who sit in judgment on us in such a high-handed way derive no political benefit.

For how is it possible, in the last analysis, to give credence to the accusations about our alleged desire to "absorb", to "monopolise", to exercise "dictatorship", seeing that when we were strongest and when temptations of that kind might have had most appeal for us—during our war—the government was in fact headed by socialists, enjoying our support?

While a socialist was Prime Minister and socialists held the Ministries of Defence, Air and the Navy, the Interior, Foreign Affairs, Economic Affairs, and Justice—that is to say, all the Ministries with the most power—we had only the Ministry of Agriculture and, alternately, the Ministry of Labour and that of Education.

We never used our strength—although that strength was real and effective—to demand more posts in the government. We never attempted to make capital out of Soviet aid—the only real aid the Republic had—so as to put forward demands of that kind. And even if we did have two Ministries, that was only because we acceded to the wishes of the Socialist Party, and not because we asked for them or made our support or our contribution to the struggle conditional on participation in the government.

It is necessary to face up to the problems of the present and the future. If what is desired is to put an end to the Franco dictatorship and to establish democracy, if what is desired is to proceed towards socialism, how can that be reconciled with a crude and virulent anti-communism?

Spanish politics are beginning to make a turn, to take a new starting point. We must put aside the stereotyped attitudes of the past and concentrate on the new prospects. This has two aspects.

The first is that which opens up with regard to the transition from dictatorship to democracy. In order to bring this to pass without producing once again a situation involving violence, *a minimum agreement is needed among the broadest selection of forces—an agreement which will give formal expression to an undertaking to settle political quarrels within the framework of genuinely democratic institutions. No one should be excluded a priori from the right to take part in public life within this framework. The only ones who will exclude themselves will be those who do not accept it, who cling to the dictatorship in an effort to prolong it at all costs. Within this framework the rights of all groups, the strong and the weak, should be respected. Those of the Left and those of the Right. It is clear that to get such a result it is necessary to throw out the catchwords of civil war, the set-ups that have been dominant throughout these years. The people's right freely to elect those who govern them must be recognised.*

The second aspect of the new prospects opens the way towards the culmination and further development of that system of political liberties, with the attainment of economic democracy through the reduction of privileges and finally the suppression of the financial and landowning oligarchy. The democratic and peaceful advance towards this system will require the aid of all the progressive forces which, united, will thus be laying the foundations for the socialist society of the future.

19

We communists do not conceal the fact that we are resolved to proceed to socialism, even though that is not something which will happen tomorrow.

We would never accept a commitment which would tie us to the present social system; what we are prepared to agree to, the commitment we are prepared to undertake and uphold, is that which refers to respect for, and the defence of, democratic liberties, but not on any account of the capitalist system.

Let us see what our attitude is towards some of the most important problems involved in creating that new climate in our country's political and social relations.

A NEW LOOK AT THE RELATIONS BETWEEN THE PROGRESSIVE FORCES, THE CHURCH AND CATHOLICISM

The Integrist Tradition and the Anti-clerical Tradition

One of the most burning questions, for the whole of the Left, is that of the Church and the Catholic movement. Traditions here are very much alive and do not readily give way. Behind, there is a long and dark history. Ever since the time when the nobility and the Church united in order to expel the Moors and carry out the *Reconquista*, Catholicism has been an instrument of state policy. First of all with the feudal aristocracy, and later, when that class and the bourgeoisie came to an understanding, the Church made a decisive contribution in the suppression of any attempts at reform. The enfeoffment of the Church to the reactionary state continues to this day; following Vatican Council Two, Franco continues to reserve for himself the right to name the bishops, and they—with the exception of a minority who deserve our respect—are without any real independence in face of the fascist temporal power.

Historically speaking, therefore, the democratic forces have always come up against the Church when they have tried to remove the reactionary forces from power. The Church and the hosts it has influenced have constituted the shock forces of reaction.

Sometimes heretics were burned and at other times monasteries, convents and churches went up in flames.

Clerical reaction has traditionally pronounced the most violent anathemas against liberals, progressive people and Freemasons, and in modern times against socialists and communists. On the other hand, the progressive forces have attacked the Church, sometimes allowing their attention to be diverted from more important and more dangerous enemies.

The last of these tragic clashes was the civil war of 1936–39. The Bishops, with the exception of Monsignor Múgica and Monsignor Vidal y Barraquer, one Basque and the other Catalan, called on the clergy and the masses of Catholics to rise up against the Republic, supporting Franco. In a notorious collective letter the *war of the rich against the poor* was described as a *"crusade to defend Christianity against communism"*. In those days the Bishops raised their arms in the fascist salute and had their photographs taken in that posture for publication in the press. With the exception of the Basque clergy and their congregations and a few personalities in other parts of Spain, the Church and the Catholic movement were wholly on the side of fascism.

That explains the anti-clericalism in the Republican camp and the extreme way in which it manifested itself in many cases.

Subsequently the regime and the Church have continued to be mingled together and intertwined. The reaction against this understanding has been so deep that it has penetrated and broadened out within the Catholic world itself, to an extent never previously known in Spain. A Catholic anti-clericalism has been growing. In the movements of Catholic workers and Catholic youth there started what can be regarded, to a certain degree, as a revolt against integrism and collusion with the regime. The same thing happened among the clergy—among the young clergy and among sections of the older ones, and also among some

21

members of the Church hierarchy. The actions of Pope John XXIII, the Encyclical *"Pacem in terras"*, and then the Vatican Council, helped to give confidence and encouragement to this reforming section. The top hierarchy of the Spanish Church found itself compelled to make some tentative gestures signifying reserve with regard to the regime, without, however, making any fundamental change in its fundamental line. *Even now that hierarchy has not yet made the gesture of declaring itself publicly in favour of a measure so elementary, judged from the purely Christian point of view as well, as the amnesty.* There are Bishops who continue to act as hangers-on of Franco in the phantasmagorical Cortes of procurators. While the government is nullifying the project for religious freedom, timidly inspired by the agreements of the Vatican Council, the members of the church hierarchy are supporting this with their silence. The famous Plan XIII, as far as they are concerned, might never have been approved. When the police take action against priests who offer to testify in favour of what is upheld in that plan, the top hierarchy abandons them and, to all intents and purposes, reproves their action. Lastly, in a situation in which there is a recrudescence of repression against the democratic forces, the top hierarchy not only gives the seal of approval to this with its silence, but collaborates by carrying out its own repression against the militant members of Catholic Action—council members and conciliar clergy. The removal of the editors of *Signo* by the Episcopal Assembly is one of the most scandalous episodes in that repression.

In face of conduct of this kind how have the communists behaved? Obviously, we have criticised the policy of the reactionary members of the church hierarchy. How could we have refrained from doing so? Nevertheless, side by side with this, we have done everything humanly possible to help our people to overcome the sectarian attitudes of the past and to fill in the ditch that was dug, and not by us, between believers and democracy. When Monsignor Guerra Campos made a speech in the Council—a speech with which, let it be said, his subsequent behaviour has had little in common—we published it in one of our reviews and commented favourably on it. It was a question of a Bishop, a member of the top hierarchy. Our attitude to that speech shows that it is not our aim to stir up strife between Catholics and the members of their hierarchy. What we want, and what many Catholic laymen and priests also want, is that the positions of the hierarchy should evolve, in harmony with the *aggiornamento*. We could have adopted another attitude. We could have taken advantage of the responsibility incurred by the Church in relation to the Franco regime in order to attack the Church as a whole. Who would have blamed us for that? We should have been continuing the traditional line of the Left against the reactionary character of the Church. Neither *Ecclesia* nor the newspapers of the *Editorial Católica* publishing house over which Monsignor Herrera presides with all his authority, would have attacked us more than they are now doing.

It is not in our interest, however, to help the Catholic integrists, the reactionaries who cannot tell the difference between the altar and Franco's throne, preserve the Church for an indefinite period as an instrument of reaction. If we had attacked the Church as a whole, we should have played into the hands of the integrists. They would certainly prefer it if we communists and the Left were to wave the old anti-clerical banner; they would prefer it if we called for the burning of churches and monasteries so that they could go back easily to mixing up reaction and religion, counter-revolution and a crusade! They are more "churchmen" than "Christians".

When we advocate understanding and brotherhood between communists and Catholics in order to make this "vale of tears" more habitable; when we welcome the democratic stand of certain members of the hierarchy, priests and laymen, and salute the honest attitude of Catholic militants—workers, priests and intellectuals; when we look with a favourable eye at the *aggiornamento* and affirm our desire to respect Catholic sentiments and the activity of the Church in its specific sphere; when we strive to surmount the violence and the conflicts of the past, the integrists answer us with the childish fable about the wolf and the lamb—they who have so often acted as wolves against the people and who act as wolves against their own fellow Catholics from the moment when the latter cease to accept the reactionary policy and the mixing up of the Church with the dictatorship.

Who is it that does more harm to the Church and Spanish Catholicism—those of us who are advocating an attitude of respect towards them, or the members of the hierarchy who persist in turning their backs on the present and the future and dream of reviving the days when Spain was "the hammer of the heretics"?

We declared quite a long time ago that we are not ready to fall for the provocation of the integrist section of the Church hierarchy. We are not going to move into the terrain of sectarianism and violence, we are not going to stoke the flames of any conflagration. A reform movement has arisen within the Church and is trying naturally to impart new life to it but, at the same time, trying to give it a new spirit and to free it from the domination of the ruling classes and from the use they have made of it as one of their instruments; trying to overcome the Constantinian temptation; to go forward along the path of the *aggiornamento* and of progress. That movement is coming up against difficulties, against strong resistance. In spite of its considerable importance, it is in a minority in the Church, though not perhaps in the Catholic world. It is travelling along a thorny path which resembles in some ways the one which we communists are following in the fight for freedom. And so, therefore, in defining our attitude to the Church and to Spanish Catholicism, we prefer to take as our reference that movement to which the future belongs, and not the integrist *ultras,* who, like Francoism, are condemned by history. It is an option which, to certain people on the Left with traditional out-looks, may seem risky and dangerous. "And what if the *ultras* succeed in crushing the progressives?"—That is one of the objections that is made. If the *ultras* crush the progressives, that can mean the prolongation of the existence of an additional cause of tension in Spanish society. But in the long run it is not we who will be the losers; it will be the Church itself which will have crushed the only forces which, in reforming it, can prolong and maintain its influence among broad sections of the people.

Passions must be cooled and the political struggle in Spain must be freed from religious interference! That is one of the preconditions for creating that new political and social climate which we are advocating and which Spain needs.

The so-called "Church of Silence"

The integrists—and in some cases not only the integrists but also certain other ill-informed Catholics—sometimes blame us for the situation which is referred to—less and less every day, it is true—as the *Church of Silence*. In answer to them we could say that the most convincing example of the *Church of Silence*—of silence in face of oppression, injustice and abuses perpetrated by those who wield power—is the one represented by the majority of our Bishops. But we do not refuse to deal with this question calmly and objectively, especially when we are speaking to Catholics who have honest doubts and who say to us: "We are in agreement with you when you speak about living together, about mutual respect and about collaboration, but what is going on in the communist countries?"

In this or that country which is governed by communists, what is happening is more or less what might happen in Spain supposing that a socialist revolution were to triumph there in face of a Church led by Franco bishops like the present ones, with a semi-feudal and semi-capitalist mentality, regarding socialism as a diabolical form of society which had to be denounced and destroyed in the name of the faith.

There is no doubt that co-existence between an integrist Church and socialism is a hard and difficult problem. That is the principal cause of many of the conflicts that arise between Church and State in some of the socialist countries, where the Church, on account of that orientation, transforms itself into the main instrument of the social groups which hope to achieve the restoration of capitalism.

The Hungarian Church and the members of its hierarchy whom it inherited from the days of the Horthy dictatorship, were, under the leadership of Cardinal Mindszenty, a very clear example of an integrist Church that upheld the old forms of society. The same could be said about Vishinsky's Polish Church which, in the Vatican Council, together with a large section of the members of Spanish hierarchy, took its place in the ranks of the integrists.

Notwithstanding those attitudes, the Church functions in freedom in those countries and receives subsidies from the state. The conflicts with the state are tending to be overcome, and would already have been finally overcome had it not been for the reactionary incursions in the political field in which some of the church dignitaries indulge from time to time.

The problem is whether the Church can cease to identify itself, as an institution, with the capitalist system. Following Pope John and the Second Vatican Council, a trend has been initiated which can proceed in this direction. This constitutes the key to co-operation between the socialist state and the Catholic Church or any other Church. The co-existence, and also the collaboration—in the case of the war against Hitlerism and the fight for peace—between the Soviet State and the Orthodox Church, are a positive example, showing that this is possible.

In making a critical examination of the experience acquired in relations between Church and State in the socialist countries, there is no doubt that we communists, too, can draw useful lessons for our present and future

26

conduct with regard to the Church.

In defining our attitude, we communists take into account the new prospects opened up by Pope John XXIII and the Vatican Council. We want to take these as our starting point rather than the struggles of the past and the passions which those struggles have left in their wake. These prospects indicate the possibility of an alliance between communists, socialists, Christians and other forces for the defence of peace; the possibility that the Church will not stand, collectively, in the way of progress and socialism. Today there is talk of the *other priests*, meaning by that those who stand for the new conciliar trends. In this sense we could speak of the *other Church*—that which expresses itself as the Catholic publicist Enrique Miret Magdalena has done in the following terms :

"In face of the socialist reality of the world today we ought to meditate, as the Benedictine Sebastian Moore has done, admitting that 'it constitutes the first effective attempt, since the feudal system, to establish a complete human society, and the ease with which we go on to condemn that attempt on the basis of theological principles, should be a danger signal for us'."

No Catholic should take offence when we speak about the *other Church*. By this we mean, not only a different social stand, not committed to a society divided into exploiting and exploited classes, but also a less primitive, more conciliar attitude in religious propaganda. The ways in which the Church, at certain moments, has tried to wrench the masses away from revolutionary influences, having recourse to fantastic tales, exorcisms and spectacular demonstrations designed to arouse superstition and primitive passions rather than religious feeling, do not help to promote the relations between historic movements which aim, the one from political and social foundations and the other from religious ones, to go beyond capitalist society.

In the same way we communists ought to take care not to get involved in the likewise primitive forms which atheist

27

propaganda has managed to assume at certain times, forgetting the profound observation made by Engels :

"A religion that brought the Roman world empire into subjection and dominated by far the greater part of civilized humanity for 1,800 years cannot be disposed of merely by declaring it to be nonsense gleaned together by frauds."— (Bruno Bauer and Early Christianity)

To sum up, what I want to say is that in Spain it is not *fatally inevitable* that there must be a repetition, between democracy—and in the future between socialism—and the Church, either of the conflicts which occurred in the past or of those which may arise today in certain socialist countries. Experience can and should be of assistance to both sides. But if this is to be so, then it is necessary for both sides to work to change the climate in which their mutual relations have developed in the past and are still developing now. That is what we in our sphere, and the conciliar Catholic tendencies in theirs, are endeavouring to do in Spain. For us, from our point of view, it is a fundamental question to take *a new look* at the problem of relations with the Church and the Catholic world. They, from their point of view, are faced with the same problem.

In this connection, we regard with every sympathy the break in the traditional isolation between socialist countries and the Vatican. The fact that statesmen, communists, like Comrade Podgorny, have had interviews with the Pope; that Cuba maintains normal relations with the Vatican and that Yugoslavia is resuming relations—these seem to us to be steps in the right direction, which do not signify any ideological abdication but which come within the scope of that *new look*—more up-to-date, realistic and favourable to human interests—at the relations between socialism and the Church.

We do not underestimate the difficulties which still stand in the way of this; but the difficulties ought not to make us give up. We have to record, and at the same time help to proclaim, a series of new events which should be taken into account when we are defining our attitude.

The trends making towards theological renewal are acquiring fresh strength. The simplified and primitive God of the catechism, the God of resignation on Earth and felicity in Heaven, presented for centuries by the Church, could not satisfy believers living in an epoch when man is going out into the cosmos and when, with his work and his science, he can perform what would earlier have been regarded as a miracle; in an epoch in which marvellous means of communication, although in a fragmentary way and with much mystification, are helping to bring knowledge and culture to the broad masses of the people. A whole series of dogmatic structures which shored up the "good conscience" of Catholics exercising power and the resignation of Catholics living in poverty, have come toppling to the ground.

According to the decisions of Vatican Council II, capitalism and a society divided into exploited and exploiting classes have ceased to be regarded by the Church as the immutable natural order of things, against which it is a sin to rebel.

I do not know if everyone is aware of what these changes mean for Spain. But perhaps it may be sufficient, in order to get somewhere near to their exact significance, to say that if they had taken place before 1936, Franco's military "putsch" would not have occurred, or, in any event, would never have been transformed into civil war. And if, to embark on hypotheses, a Council similar to Vatican II had been held in the days of the great French Revolution, there would have been no burning of monasteries in Spain. All of that, naturally, belongs to the realm of speculation, but it does serve to present in a more graphic way the significance which the changes that have taken place within the Church can have for Spain.

In opening ourselves up to the Catholic movement we do not depart from our class position—we maintain it. There is no need to recall that in the past, when conditions were

29

not the same and the Catholic movement, fundamentally speaking, identified itself with reaction—already at that time the Communist Party, on the basis of its Marxist-Leninist stand, combated the petit-bourgeois anti-clericalism which regarded the dissolution of the Jesuits as the supreme culmination of revolutionary measures, while it left intact the power of finance capital, the landowning aristocracy and the old state machine.

In his work "The Attitude of the Workers' Party towards Religion", Lenin recalled that :

"Engels . . . frequently condemned the efforts of people who desired to be 'more Left' or 'more revolutionary' than the Social Democrats to introduce an explicit avowal of atheism, in the sense of declaring war on religion, into the programme of the workers' party."—*Marx-Engels-Marxism*, p. 274.

Today, however, the problem presents itself on different ground, and much more clearly. Between communists and Catholics there is beginning to disappear—and we should like it to disappear completely, in which connection our "open" position is also very important—the barrier which used to be constituted by religion, manipulated as an instrument of the ruling classes against any revolutionary policy. Religion, conceived and employed in that way, was a powerful weapon for dividing the toiling classes; it transformed part of them into mass reserves of finance capital and the great landowners. The policy of the unity of the toiling classes stopped, in the decade of the 'thirties, although much against our will, at that barrier. Today not only we, but the conciliar Catholics as well, are striving to raze it to the ground. How can we fail to appreciate the full importance of this fact, which can play a fundamental role in opening up a sure way towards democracy and socialism?

The union of the people, the alliance between the forces of labour and culture, cannot be achieved in Spain if the Catholic working people and intellectuals are excluded.

From what has been said, it follows that we envisage a

chosen field for the collaboration of Catholics, communists and other democratic forces : the social and political field, i.e., the "plan of practical achievements" to which Pope John XXIII referred in his Encyclical. It is clear that this collaboration will not be possible with *all* Catholics, but only with those who take a democratic or progressive stand. Many—if not all, then nearly all—of the members of the financial and landowning oligarchy call themselves Catholics. Nevertheless, there is no possibility of collaboration between them, as a class, and us. But thousands of Catholics are in the same situation as we are, and they include not a few priests, who may concur with those of whom we have just spoken, in church, at the time of Mass, without concurring with them in any way in the political and social field.

In this connection we do not hide the fact that what is important in the first place is that religion should not divide the people—to use expressions favoured by some members of the hierarchy—into hungry and militant *wolves* and meek and mild *lambs. Ecclesia's* reply to the statements I made to *Le Figaro* and *l'Unitá* is in fact imbued with the desire to go on using religion as a means of dividing the people. I do not believe that it delights the hearts of the mass of Catholics today to go on being treated like a flock of sheep in need of shepherds, which has to be protected from *wolves*. Those similes might have been comprehensible in the days when the job of shepherd was one of the more common and more remunerative occupations; nowadays they clash with the concept of democracy and the natural tendency of the masses of working people to occupy the leading place in society which is rightfully theirs. It is quite understandable that as far as the Franco regime is concerned, it is anxious that Catholics and communists should not get together or act together. We do not understand, however, what interest the Church, as an institution that is not temporal in character, can have in this.

Perhaps it may interest the editors of *Ecclesia* to know

31

that in the ranks of the Left there are also diehards who talk in much the same way as they themselves do and who, when we communists pursue a policy of holding out our hands to the Catholics, warn us : "Take care! Don't be naive. The men in black are wolves. Now they have disguised themselves as sheep, but as soon as they get the chance they will gobble you up."

While the Catholic "ultras" talk about monasteries and convents being burned down and about the persecution of religion, "our" sectarian individuals, for their part, are not short of arguments and reasons; on the contrary, they have more than enough. Without needing to go back as far as the burnings of the Inquisition, they remember that in their own village, in 1936, the fascists concealed weapons in the church and fired from the church tower with machine-guns; they recall the frenzied priests who hastened to take up arms against the Republic, fighting rifle in hand. They recall those who, with their crucifixes, broke the teeth of dying men who would not agree to make confession. They have not forgotten the monasteries which were converted into prisons, the long years of repression with the connivance of the Church; the collective letter of the Bishops in June 1937, the collaboration between the Church and fascism and so many other things !

Nor have we ourselves forgotten those events, which were unhappily very grievous. Very well then, we, and the representatives of Spanish Catholicism, have to put to ourselves in all seriousness the following problem : For our relations today and in the future, are we going to take that past as our starting point? Are we going to carry on that "tradition"? Are we going to return to the "crusades" and the burning of monasteries?

We communists repudiate any return to that past. In the Church and in the Catholic camp there are considerable forces, even though they are in a very small minority in the top hierarchy, who think the same. The currents that are influencing the Vatican Council are flowing in this direction.

For Spain these phenomena are happy omens.

The collaboration between Catholics and communists in the social and political field, which is beginning to be a reality in spite of all those ridiculous fables about "wolves" and "lambs", has made a decisive contribution towards initiating the process of overcoming the historical antagonisms between the Church and democracy. The human relations and class solidarity between communists and Catholics have overthrown many barriers. It is our ardent and sincere desire to continue to take our stand on this ground and from it to open up the new stage in history which is announcing itself in Spain. For our part, I want to insist, it is not a question of a stratagem of war, nor is it a tactical position, but an orientation which I shall call strategic in order to indicate its entire profundity and importance.

Two Churches

We communists do not believe that anything is immutable. Everything changes. Spanish history has very frequently shown us the Church linked up with, if not heading, all the reactionary causes. Those whom I have described as sectarian elements of the Left think that this will go on happening from this day forth and for evermore, or for at least as long as religion continues to exist. The wounds of history continue to affect them deeply. Nevertheless, Christianity has not always taken on the same forms, nor has it always played the same role. Engels explains it in this way :

"The history of early Christianity presents notable points of resemblance with the modern working-class movement. Like the latter, Christianity was originally a movement of the people; it first appeared as the religion of slaves and emancipated slaves, of poor people deprived of all rights, of peoples subjugated or dispersed by Rome. Both Christianity and the workers' socialism preach forthcoming salvation from bondage and misery; Christianity places salvation in

33

a life beyond, after death, in Heaven; socialism places it in this world, in a transformation of society. Both are persecuted and baited and their supporters are despised and made the objects of exclusive laws. . . .

"The parallel between the two historic phenomena forces itself on our attention as early as the Middle Ages in the first risings of the oppressed peasants and particularly of the town plebians. Those risings, like all the mass movements of the Middle Ages, were bound to wear the mask of religion and appeared as the restoration of early Christianity from spreading degeneration. . . . This appeared most splendidly in the organisation of the Bohemian Taborites under John Zizka . . . but this trait pervades the whole of the Middle Ages, until it gradually fades away after the German Peasant War, to revive again with the working men Communists after 1830. The French revolutionary Communists, as also Weitling and his supporters, referred to early Christianity. . . ."

(Engels, "On the History of Early Christianity")

Constantinism made of Christianity the instrument of an oppressor state and initiated the "conservatisation" of this movement, but, as Engels explains, many subsequent revolutionary movements still took over the formulas of primitive Christianity.

In the present period, the sharpening of the contradictions between decadent capitalist imperialism and socialism, which is on the upgrade, is taking the class struggle into the bosom of the Church and of the Catholic movement. The Catholic working people are no longer prepared to resign themselves to things as they are, and they have the understanding and support of many Catholic intellectuals. The class struggle is beginning to be looked upon as a natural phenomenon, inherent in the present society. In a way that is understandable, those oppressed sections of society which follow the Church are turning towards the prophetic and rebellious Christianity of the earliest days and are selecting from it part of the reasoning which enables them to

34

harmonise the old beliefs and the new militant attitudes.

Referring to this situation, the distinguished theologian Don José González Ruiz* has written the following :

"Despite the undoubted preponderance of the Constantinian tendency in Spanish Catholicism, there has welled up, from the very depths of our religious reality, a very strong prophetic tendency. The tumultuous irruption of the prophetic tendency has brought out sharply a fact, at once painful and rich in hope, which, as experience shows, it is useless to conceal : within Spanish Catholicism *there are two Churches.*"

According to Father González Ruiz, what divides the two Churches is :

". . . a fundamental attitude in face of social, economic and political facts. *The established Church is attached to the social and economic reality in the country, confining itself to preaching individual salvation, whereas the conciliar Church regards it as its duty vigorously to condemn the existing situation, which it considers, because of its structure, to be immoral.*"

In actual fact, this view dovetails with Pope John's idea about the *Church of the poor*; Father González Ruiz is taking up a position similar to that of Monsignor Edelby, the Bishop of Damascus, when the latter, upholding the new conciliar ideas, declares that "theology cannot be the privilege of *one class in the Church.*"

It must be said that within the existing Catholic movement in Spain, in the broad section of it which is progressive, memories of the prophetic and militant spirit of early Christianity manifest themselves in a definite condemnation

* A member of the group formed in 1949 for the study of ecclesiastical sciences by the present auxiliary Archbishop of Madrid. Author of *Marxism, Christianity and the New Man*, and other works. With a group of Catholic and Protestant theologians, he prepared an ecumenical edition of the New Testament which was published in one million copies for Spanish-speaking countries.

of capitalist property. For instance, the AST,* which is Catholic in inspiration, declares that "the full human advancement of the working man is incompatible with the concept of capitalist property" and advocates :

"Social property, which may put an end to the wage system and which will correspond to all those forms of wealth which can result in exploitation of the community on the part of its owners.

"Private property in the case of all those possessions for use and consumption which are necessary for the normal development of every person and every family."

That is what makes it possible for us communists to speak of our *Catholic brothers*—without, of course, meaning by this the bankers and the big entrepreneurs who call themselves Catholics—just as we have spoken and continue to speak of our *socialist brothers*, without having in mind, when we say that, either Noske, or Scheidemann, or Tanner. In those Catholics whom we do have in mind there is neither resignation nor submission; the religion they profess is no longer precisely what Marx called the opium of the people.

Is it a question of a new dimension of religion, of its purification, as the Catholics probably think, or of a stage in the long march towards the overcoming of all religious alienation? We Marxists are inclined towards the second explanation. But the essential question here and now is not to elucidate that question, but to recognise a fact : that the religion which is the bearer of a Catholic current that comes out actively against the dictatorship, against capitalist society, and intends to contribute towards the transformation of society, is already not acting as an opiate and objectively constitutes a progressive ferment.

Marx, in his *Critique of Hegel's Philosophy of Law*, said that "the criticism of religion is . . . in embryo the criticism of the vale of tears, the halo of which is religion."

In order to succeed in formulating a radical and ruthless

* *Alianza Sindical de Trabajadores*, a Catholic trade union movement which is active in the Workers' Commissions.

critique of this "vale of tears", philosophy had to carry the critique of religion to its conclusion. It was impossible to conceive of the movement of social revolution without a firm vanguard which had been freed from religious alienation and was capable, because of that, "of unmasking self-alienation in its non-sacred forms", that is to say, of standing up to the reality of capitalism and putting an end to it. But the conclusion should not be drawn from this that what was a precondition for the philosophy which had to arm the party of the vanguard—to dismantle the mechanism of the religious alienation of man so as to enable him to face up to social reality without blinkers—should also be a precondition for the participation of all working people, the majority of the people, in the struggle for socialism. Broad masses of the people are taking part in the struggle for socialism without giving up their religious beliefs, and in certain circumstances they can derive from these beliefs the moral strength to take part in the struggle. While poverty and exploitation exist, while war and the threat of wars have not been eliminated and as long as there are people who live in dread of the present and the future and science has not become the possession of the broad masses of the people, a section of them will continue to find a refuge and a form of protest against the tribulations of real life in religious feeling.

The fundamental, the decisive thing, so that human beings may transcend the religious phenomenon, is the transformation of the socio-economic structures, and not simply the abolition of capitalism, but also the broad development, the expansion and the magnificent flourishing of new structures and of science and culture throughout the world. Because of this, atheist propaganda, on its own, will never put an end to religion and may have, in certain forms and conditions, results which are the opposite of what is intended. Still less will administrative measures put an end to religion.

It is certain that if an end is to be put to unjust social and economic structures, the solution cannot be other than revolutionary action carried to its ultimate conclusions and that such revolutionary action is inconceivable without a vanguard inspired by a revolutionary ideology, that is to say, by Marxism-Leninism. From this, and not from Catholicism, has come the radical critique of capitalist society and effective action to bring about its transformation.

In this connection we are not being guilty of conceit if we regard the radical attitude of important sections of Catholicism as a phenomenon that to a considerable extent can be attributed to the victories of Marxism, which has changed the face of the world and consequently altered the "inverted reflection of the latter" which, according to Marx's formula, religion is. This does not imply any denial of the fact that social progress in general and the extraordinary conquests of science have played and are continuing to play a very important role in the same direction.

Taking as our basis the reality of those two Churches, it is necessary to get clear on our attitude towards Catholicism. In this sphere and referring specifically to Spain, it is clear that "the established Church", which "is attached to the social and economic reality of the country, confining itself to preaching individual salvation", is the bearer of an alienating religion which acts on the people like a drug, whereas the other Church, the one which "vigorously condemns the existing situation", the one which promotes "a prophetic tendency", is a factor making for progress. This is borne out by examples like "Operation Moses" and the many activities in the sphere of political and social action which are undertaken by those who represent the second trend.

Possible Points of Agreement in Certain Spheres of Ideology
No one doubts that in the philosophical field deep divergencies exist between ourselves and this section of the "prophetic Church", between Marxism and religion. And I say in the philosophical field because it is there that the divergencies are fundamental and concrete, and because it

is necessary to define clearly the areas of possible agreement and disagreement. It is my belief that no one will be scandalised if I add that on other aspects of ideology a complete identity of judgment may be reached. For instance, political economy also forms part of ideology and in this sphere a considerable part of this Catholic sector comes out in support of the economic forms of socialism and accepts Marx's critique of the capitalist economy. It is worth emphasising that something similar happened some time ago with the followers of another of the religious families of worldwide importance—Islam. Politics also belongs to the field of ideology and it is certain that ideological agreement between those Catholics and ourselves can likewise be brought about in the sphere of the political structures of democracy and socialism. In actual fact, if points of ideological agreement in those spheres are not yet observed on the broadest scale, the reasons for this lie outside the realm of pure religion and arise from class motivations.

It follows from this that there are zones of Marxist-Leninist ideology in which there is possible, not simply co-existence, but concurrence, which renders practical collaboration more feasible.

In actual fact these points of agreement do not arise from the existence of a "Christian socialism", a copy of feudal ideology, which was criticised by Marx. A "Christian socialism" does not really exist. These points of agreement reflect the approach of sections of Catholicism to the only genuine socialism—the scientific socialism of Marx and Lenin.

In the sphere of the battle of ideas we Marxists cannot be indifferent to the phenomenon of a theological search and investigation inspired, on the one hand, by historical social and scientific progress, and on the other, by the new factors to which the contrast with the integrist Church conjures up before what we shall continue to call the prophetic Church —a search and investigation to which the Assembly has given fresh impetus. Inasmuch as that is a human problem, of concern to men and women, and a problem which affects social development in one way or another and has repercussions on our own activities, this phenomenon is of great interest to us.

For instance, when Monsignor Edelby explains the need to undertake a theological search and declares that ". . . it is necessary at all costs to defend throughout the entire Church freedom of expression, provided that it is sincere" and that "it is better to make a mistake while seeking than to stop seeking for fear of making a mistake" we have to recognise and value his subjective intention of seeking for the truth.

When Father González Ruiz speaks of a *"theology* of labour", we can attach more or less value to his variations on the religious theme of transcendence, but we do welcome some of his statements : "Grace does not come to take the place of, or fill the role of, *the autonomy and effectiveness of human labour. The Christ-event is not an extrinsic norm which renders useless the hazardous inventiveness of mankind's conscious evolution. . . .* The Christian, despite the assurance of his faith, *sincerely shares with other men and women the risks of progressive autocreation* and participates with the same anxiety and the same astonishment at the novelty of his own discovery."

We cannot adopt the idea of transcendence. What Catholics attribute to the Divine will is for Marxists that sphere of historical initiative which escapes from the individual will and individual decision, because it is shaped by the collision of many different and contradictory wills, themselves determined by specific material conditions which the individual in isolation is unable to control or counteract, and which, when he is religious, he explains by an all-powerful transcendental will to which he surrenders himself with resignation.

But the positive declarations of Father González Ruiz about the *autonomy* of *human labour,* the *conscious evolution of mankind, progressive autocreation,* contain an affirmation of the role of man as the creator of his own history, which approaches our own conception and can bring Catholics and communists closer together in common action.

In the same way, modern theological trends are daily making more and more room for human science, not only in historical development, but in explaining how the species arose. A Catholic writer has the following to say about the need for a critical interpretation of the Bible, and specifically of the Book of Genesis :

"It is science that has the floor; and today it seems to be leaning more and more towards a plural solution, with various couples at the beginning of the human species, through the evolution of the body starting from the *primates* and passing through some intermediate link."

Enrique Miret Magdalena, from whom that passage is taken, is concerned lest religious outlooks and dogmas should "be in perpetual conflict" "with historical or natural science" and with reason itself.

It can be argued that the concern of religion to come to terms with science and not to engage in conflict with it is not new and that Marx paid considerable attention to it. But in other epochs that concern led to scientific investigation being restricted—there is the example of Galileo—or to scientific explanations being kept within restricted circles so that they did not reach the people and thus no conflict between reason and faith arose in their minds. Today, on the other hand, the progressive section of Catholicism rejects any restrictions on science and maintains that it is necessary to revise those religious notions which are in contradiction with it. It is an attempt to remove the faith from the area of conflict with science so as to preserve it in a kind of personal ethical enclosure.

It is clear that when it is placed within these boundaries, the philosophical polemic between Catholics and communists is relieved of many concepts which, in the past, tended to make it more painful. Recognition of the role of man's labour and that of science in social development already provides on the ideological level, together with the points of agreement in the political and economic fields, a substantial basis of agreement for going forward together towards new historical horizons, including socialism.

There still remain other ideological divergencies the importance of which cannot be underestimated: the very existence of God, which we deny and which the Catholics affirm. The discussion on this will probably not cease for a long time to come. Nevertheless, discussion alone is not going to provide us with the solution. On the other hand, without this meaning that we are giving up propaganda for our own overall conception of the world, and without it signifying any underestimation of the overall character of our ideology, it is clear that denying the existence of God is not the paramount task of the Communist Party. Lenin in his day recalled Engels' idea that "... *proclaiming war on religion as a political mission of the workers' party is a mere anarchist pose.*" Our paramount task is the revolution, socialism, communism.

As we understand it, God will disappear from men's minds when the world ceases to be a "vale of tears", when mankind lives a happy and tranquil life, without fears or afflictions, and when science has become the heritage of the masses of the people.

Catholics, naturally, do not think so. They believe, on the contrary, that those conditions will fully reveal to human beings the true worth and reality of God.

We are convinced that our ideas are correct. They have faith in their ideas.

Time, experience and life will provide the final answer!

Meanwhile we can and should devote all our common efforts to the work of making this world here below more habitable for human beings.

For this purpose it is necessary to provide full guarantees of religious freedom for one another. The Catholics, like those who believe in other religions, must have the opportunity to practice their religion without any obstacles; we

42

ourselves, and all who regard themselves as atheists, must have the right to live and think as such and to uphold our own conceptions.

This is our proposal to the Catholics, and it coincides with the one which, some time ago, Father Cafarena made to us. That is the orientation which, already today, inspires our collaboration with broad sections of Catholics.

No political manoeuvre is involved in this. We insist on this statement in face of the stupid charges of the integrists, in face of the fable about *wolves* and *lambs*. But it is also valid and opportune for not a few people in our camp who continue to be obsessed by the attitude of the Church in the not distant past and by the fact that this attitude is being maintained in the present conduct of the top hierarchy and many of its followers.

Nor is it a tactic inspired by short-term political objectives.

We ourselves must realise that it is a question of a new look at the entire historical prospect for progress in our country, of a new way of behaving with regard to the Catholic question and, in general, the phenomenon of religion.

Having said this, we are not blind to the difficulties which this orientation will still have to overcome. We are still coming up against them. The conciliar Catholics are also coming up against them, and more directly than we are.

They are being blamed, almost as if for a crime, for engaging in a dialogue and collaborating with communists and they are being condemned for addressing us as "communist brothers". Every day they get it thrown in their faces that the victory of socialism in other countries has been accompanied by collisions between the new power and the Church. And they are being called on to model their attitude in Spain towards the communists on what has characterised the Church in those countries.

Cannot things happen differently in Spain? We communists declare that they can and we sincerely and deeply want them to happen differently.

Whether things happen in Spain differently from in other countries does not depend solely on our attitude; it depends on that prophetic Church, of which González Ruiz speaks, succeeding in getting Spanish Catholicism to create, here and now, relations of understanding with the advanced forces of society. It depends on the foundations for collaboration being laid now, and on sectarian nations fading away on both sides, on the past being overcome.

Modifying a situation which has lasted for centuries may seem, at first, to be an over-ambitious task. Some people will possibly accuse us of a certain naivety, while others will accuse us of an unduly Machiavellian approach. Nor will there be any lack of people who will remember that in Spain atheist bourgeois thinkers who might have found a common basis for co-existence with the Church in the social sphere have already failed.

Nevertheless, the bourgeoisie, and still more so feudalism, as classes, have also lasted for centuries and are today on the verge of disappearing. Bourgeois atheist and democratic thought in Spain was unable to reach a basis for co-existence with the Church for the same reasons which prevented it, at one time and another, from carrying through its own revolution to the end. At a different level, in this as in other spheres, the proletariat finds itself confronted with the need to carry out tasks which the bourgeoisie was unable to complete. It is our job to overcome, on the one hand, the Inquisitorial spirit, the spirit of a "crusade", and on the other the anti-clericalism of the 1900s, and bring about a new relationship between those who believe and those who do not.

Even if the forces belonging to the conciliar sector were weaker than they actually are, we should still take the attitude which I have explained. In a country such as ours, this is the real orientation of the future. There is no other. In the last extreme, in the unlikely event of the conciliary sectors being stifled, the moral strength which that position gives us in face of the Catholic masses who want liberty and

44

progress, would be an advantage in the struggle for democracy and socialism.

What was Universal and what was purely Russian in the Soviet Revolution

We communists have declared that we are fighting for democracy; that we want to carry through the revolution and go forward to socialism along a peaceful road, and that we conceive the period of transition from capitalism to socialism, in the conditions prevailing in our country, as a democratic state, with a plurality of parties and political liberties.

Our opponents immediately reply to us in the following terms : "Yes, you say that, but that is not your doctrine; your doctrine is the dictatorship of the proletariat, one single party and the suppression of liberty for those who do not think as you do. That is the experience of the countries of the East. Where communism is victorious, liberty vanishes."

To speak sincerely, it must be admitted that these arguments also make an impression on people who are not enemies of ours, but who are, or who can be, our allies and who are looking for clarification. Our answer is not always convincing. For years, we ourselves incorporated in our conceptions, more or less as a reflex, the idea that one single party and socialism were complementary; that the dictatorship of the proletariat had to be exercised exclusively by the Marxist-Leninist party of the proletariat; that the concept of the dictatorship of the proletariat was necessarily the negation of any political rights for the bourgeoisie. In adopting that attitude we moved away from Leninism and replaced it by conceptions which did not belong to Lenin but to Stalin. We failed to distinguish between the essence of the dictatorship of the proletariat and the forms it had assumed in Russia. Stalin's error, in which we ourselves shared, consisted at this point in generalising *those forms,*

45

in making of *those forms* a theory of universal validity, losing sight of the fact that what possessed general, universal validity was only the content. In *State and Revolution* Lenin had already written something essential with regard to this point when he said : "Bourgeois states are most varied in form, but their essence is the same : all these states, whatever their form, in the final analysis, are inevitably the dictatorship of the bourgeoisie. The transition from capitalism to communism is certainly bound to yield a tremendous abundance and variety of political forms. . . ." (Collected Works, Vol. 25, p. 43.)*

Limited by this *universalisation* of the *forms* which the socialist state had taken in the U.S.S.R. for specific historical reasons, we left to our adversaries the benefit of defending political liberties in face of socialism. We appeared before our friends as the defenders of economic freedom, and we gave the impression that this was in principle incompatible, at least for a lengthy period of history, with political freedom. Consequently our struggle for political liberties, in the specific case of Spain, was denounced by our opponents as an attitude adopted to suit the circumstances of the given moment. To all appearances—and we ourselves, as a result of this limitation, helped to give rise to those appearances, which were actually contrary to the reality—our struggle for political liberties was no more than a tactical phase on the way towards the suppression of those same liberties, in order to achieve economic freedom. Nevertheless, in the sphere of doctrine—and, as we shall see presently, in that of practice, too—this does not accord with reality. In order to remove this mistaken impression, which we ourselves have helped to create, it was not, and is not sufficient to make general declarations, which might seem to be inspired by tactical considerations; what is necessary is to bring out the theoretical foundation of these declarations,

* All quotations from Lenin's Collected Works refer to the complete edition published in English by Lawrence & Wishart, London.

which have been drawn from Marxism-Leninism, and to reject and overcome the earlier deformations.

Lenin, when he was arguing in April 1917 with those whom he called the "old" Bolsheviks, because they kept on mechanically reiterating the Bolshevik formulations of 1905, wrote: *"The principal mistake which revolutionaries can make is to look backwards, towards the revolutions of the past, at a moment when life itself is bringing forward so many new elements which must be fitted into the general chain of events."* This attitude towards new developments, this refusal to see the revolutions of the present day as a schematic reproduction of those which have taken place in the past is a principle of universal validity on which we must firmly base ourselves.

The political form in which revolutions achieve victory and consolidate themselves is determined by a series of historical circumstances which do not always correspond to the wishes of the revolutionaries themselves. In the long run history takes shape through the confrontation of a series of different and opposed wills, and its outcome is never precisely, and in every aspect, what was intended even by the very forces which finally succeed in winning the victory.

In April 1917 Lenin wrote: ". . . this latest government (that of the Soviets) is the only possible revolutionary government, the only one that expresses the consciousness and the will of the workers and peasants." *"To become a power the class-conscious workers must win the majority to their side. As long as no violence is used against the people there is no other road to power. We are not Blanquists, we do not stand for the seizure of power by a minority."*— (Collected Works, Vol. 24, p. 40.)

Here Lenin unequivocally upheld the idea of coming to power by a democratic road, without having recourse to violence as long as the ruling classes did not do so and respected the rules of democracy within the Soviets, in which petit-bourgeois parties were then in the majority.

Lenin advocated the winning of a majority in the Soviets

47

through a labour of *patient persuasion*, of enlightenment; the *necessity* for power—Soviet power—and the *obligation* for communists *to submit to it*, even when they were in a minority. In this attitude there is an explicit recognition of the rules of political democracy. "We want to convince the majority of the people that power should belong exclusively to the Councils of Deputies of workers, soldiers, etc.", declared Lenin, and he said this, it must be repeated, at a time when the petit-bourgeois parties had a majority in the Soviets.

In May of the same year, the founder of the Soviet state was insisting that as long as the capitalists and their government did not employ violence against the masses, as long as the masses could freely express their will and freely elect and recall the authorities, what was essential was *"compliance with the will of the majority of the population and free criticism of this will by the discontented minority."* (Collected Works, Vol. 24, p. 200.)

The democratic and peaceful path which Lenin and the communists wanted to see the socialist revolution in Russia take, turned out to be impossible because of the attitude of the ruling classes, who closed it by resorting to violence. In June the Provisional Government started a campaign of repression against the revolutionary masses and especially against the communists. Lenin and other leaders had to go underground. Profiting by the weakening which this brought about in the democratic forces, the reactionaries, headed by General Kornilov, started an uprising against the Republic —an uprising which was defeated at the gates of Petrograd, thanks to workers mobilised and led by the communists. Arising from Kornilov's defeat, a situation was created in which the Soviets could take power, peacefully, provided that the Mensheviks and the Socialist-Revolutionaries so desired. At that moment Lenin pointed to the possibility of an alliance among the Bolsheviks, Mensheviks and Socialist-Revolutionaries "which has not yet been tried; or to be more precise . . . has been tried on *one front only*, for *five*

48

days only, from August 26 to 31, the period of the Kornilov revolt, and this alliance at that time scored a victory over the counter-revolution." (*The Russian Revolution and the Civil War*. Collected Works, Vol. 36.)

Even at the beginning of September, in his work "On Compromises", Lenin was writing :

"The Russian revolution is experiencing so abrupt and original a turn that we, as a party, may offer a voluntary compromise—true, not to our direct and main class enemy, the bourgeoisie, but to our nearest adversaries, the 'ruling' petty-bourgeois-democratic parties, the Socialist-Revolutionaries and Mensheviks."

"The compromise on our part is our return to the pre-July demand of all power to the Soviets and a government of S.R.s and Mensheviks responsible to the Soviets.

"The compromise would amount to the following : the Bolsheviks, without making any claim to participate in the government . . . would refrain from demanding the immediate transfer of power to the proletariat and the poor peasants and from employing revolutionary methods of fighting for this demand. A condition that is self-evident and not new to the S.R.s and Mensheviks would be complete freedom of propaganda and the convocation of the Constituent Assembly without further delays or even at an earlier date.

"The Mensheviks and the S.R.s, being the government bloc, would then agree (assuming that the compromise had been reached) to form a government wholly and exclusively responsible to the Soviets, the latter taking over all power locally as well. This would constitute the 'new' condition. I think the Bolsheviks would advance no other conditions, trusting that the revolution would proceed peacefully and party strife in the Soviets would be *peacefully overcome* thanks to really complete freedom of propaganda and to the immediate establishment of a new democracy in the composition of the Soviets (new elections) and in their functioning."

"The Bolsheviks would gain the opportunity of quite freely advocating their views and of trying to win influence in the Soviets under a really complete democracy." "*We* have nothing to fear from real democracy, for reality is on our side, and even the course of development of trends within the S.R. and Menshevik parties, which are hostile to us, proves us right.

"The Mensheviks and the S.R.s would gain in that they would at once obtain every opportunity to carry out *their* bloc's programme with the support of the obviously overwhelming majority of the people and in that they would secure for themselves the 'peaceful' use of their majority in the Soviets." (*On Compromises*. Collected Works, Vol. 25, pp. 306-8.)

I have copied out these very extensive quotations because they are little known among the Spanish public and provide a very clear idea of the efforts which Lenin and the Russian communists made to arrive at a peaceful road and an understanding with the social-democratic and petty-bourgeois parties and at the same time to give the Soviets a democratic and multi-party character. Developing these same ideas, Lenin wrote on September 26-27, 1917 :

"By seizing full power, the Soviets could still today— and this is probably their last chance—ensure the peaceful development of the revolution, peaceful elections of Deputies, a peaceful struggle of parties inside the Soviets; they could test the programmes of the various parties in practice and power could pass peacefully from one party to another." (*The Tasks of the Revolution*. Collected Works, Vol. 26, p. 68.)

Expressed here with complete clarity we have the conception of a multi-party socialist democracy which, if it had been achieved, would have enabled the transition to socialism to proceed along a peaceful path. The responsibility for the fact that developments took a different course rests, not with the Bolsheviks, but with the Socialist-

Revolutionaries and Mensheviks who, 40 days before the victory of the October Revolution, rejected that proposal. In the same work Lenin warned them prophetically of the consequences which this rejection would have :

"The entire course of development of the revolution, from the movement of April 20 to the Kornilov adventure, shows that there is bound to be *the bitterest civil war between the bourgeosie and the proletariat if this opportunity is missed*.

"Inevitable catastrophe will bring this war nearer. It must end, as all data and considerations accessible to human reason go to prove, in the full victory of the working class, in that class, supported by the poor peasantry carrying out the above programme; it may, however, prove very difficult and bloody; and may cost the lives of tens of thousands of landowners, capitalists and officers. . . . The proletariat will not hesitate to make every sacrifice to save the revolution. . . ."

Unfortunately the petit-bourgeois forces did not draw any lesson from events, let themselves be carried away by political blindness and submitted to the demands of the reactionary bourgeoisie, leaving power in the hands of the Provisional Government.

While the yearning for peace, bread and land was growing among the people and in the army, as also the influence of the Communist Party, the Provisional Government persisted in persecuting those who opposed its policy. It was necessary to answer the violence of the ruling classes with revolutionary violence and the Revolution triumphed, not by the peaceful road about which Lenin was thinking in April, and even in September, but by the path of insurrection.

In spite of everything, after the victory of October, the Bolsheviks continued to be ready to collaborate with the petit-bourgeois parties :

"It is not our fault", said Lenin, "that the Socialist-Revolutionaries and the Mensheviks have gone. They were invited to share political power, but they want to sit on the fence until the fight against Kerensky is over.

"We asked everyone to take part in the government. . . .
It [the Petrograd garrison] knows that *we wanted a*
coalition Soviet government. We did not exclude anyone
from the Soviet."* (Lenin's report to the representatives of
the Petrograd garrison, November 11, 1917. Collected
Works, Vol. 26, p. 269.) (My italics.—S.C.)

Shortly after the victory of the insurrection, it was not
only the communists who figured in the Soviet government;
in the government there was also the only other party which
agreed with them in making peace and in giving the land
to the peasants—the party of the Left Socialist-Revolutionaries. In a reorganisation of the government, four
months after the victory, it was again proposed that the
Mensheviks should take part. This attitude shows that *the*
Russian communists did not identify the socialist revolution
and the dictatorship of the proletariat with the government
of a single party. The socialists of the Second International
did not enter the government, simply because they did not
want to do so and, with that end in view, put forward
unacceptable demands. They put forward as a condition
for their participation the elimination of Lenin and the
principal leaders of the revolution, giving to this demand,
moreover, the significance of an open condemnation of the
October Revolution. Everything went to show that the
Mensheviks were refusing to collaborate with the revolution;
they set themselves the goal of isolating the communists in
the hope that this isolation would bring about the collapse
of Soviet power, which was their avowed aim.

The idea that Soviet power could not last was very widespread at that time. It was a question of the first socialist
revolution in the world, surrounded by powerful enemies—
all the imperialist powers—which were attacking it by
military means; confronted with immense problems, such as
hunger and economic disorganisation; with the onslaught
of internal counter-revolution which had the support of
parties that called themselves "left".

In 1918 the Left Socialist-Revolutionaries came out against the Brest-Litovsk peace and organised insurrections in Moscow and other parts of the country against the new power. On August 30 they made an attempt to assassinate Lenin and round about the same time they did assassinate the communist leaders Uritsky and Volodarsky. Because of that, the Left Socialist-Revolutionaries were outlawed. Shortly afterwards, in spite of everything, they were again allowed to function.

Even though, for the reasons already given, they were not taking part in the government, the Mensheviks and Socialist-Revolutionaries continued to enjoy a status of legality and were the *legal* opposition in the Soviets until 1921. Their presence as the legal opposition did not prevent them from taking part in all the uprisings of the White Guards and in whatever governments the latter and the interventionist armies of the Entente set up in various parts of Russia during the civil war. And if in 1921 they were outlawed once and for all, this was due to their participation in the Kronstadt counter-revolutionary uprising. A writer as opposed to the communists as Isaac Deutscher has made the following admission in one of his books : "To start with, the Bolsheviks tried to show themselves tolerant with their adversaries. In the congresses of the Soviets and of the trade unions the representatives of the Mensheviks, Socialist-Revolutionaries, syndicalists and anarchists spoke freely and energetically criticised the government." (*re-translated*) The Kronstadt insurrection, however, was the last straw. Russia, at that time, was ruined by the imperialist war, foreign intervention and civil war. Hunger was spreading through the country. Soviet power found itself forced to undertake its own defence with the greatest possible energy. Years later, when this crisis began to be overcome, the old bourgeois and petit-bourgeois parties had no one who would listen to them in the country, their *émigré* leaders had become increasingly remote and were coming more and more into conflict with the Revolution and any possibility of an agreement with them had disappeared. From then on, and because of this, the Communist Party transformed itself into the only party existing in the Soviet Union.

In the book already referred to, Isaac Deutscher recognises that "The idea that a single party should rule the Soviets was not in any way inherent in the Bolshevik programme. Still less so was the idea that only one party could exist." (*re-translated*) This testimony is all the more valuable since it comes from a political adversary of the Bolsheviks.

To talk now about what the socialist revolution would have been like if the Mensheviks, Socialist-Revolutionaries and other forces had accepted, and had participated in, the Soviet system in the capacity of parties, instead of going over to the ranks of the counter-revolution, would mean entering the realm of pure speculation. What we are anxious to bring out, in line with the reasoning here expounded, is that *Leninism as a doctrine—and as far as has been possible, in practice—signifies neither the exercise of power exclusively by the Communist Party, nor the existence of the Communist Party as the only party.*

If in practice, in the end, it happened as it did, Lenin has explained why : "Nobody drove the bourgeoisie out of the Soviets either before or after the October Revolution. The bourgeoisie themselves left the Soviets. The bourgeoisie, which was convinced that the consolidation of the Revolution was a vain illusion and that it would be sufficient to boycott the new power in order to bring about its downfall." —(Collected Works, Vol. 29, p. 185.)

The first socialist revolution in the world found itself in a situation in which its forces were vastly inferior to those of capitalism. It was, as it were, the head of the battering ram of world revolution. And this head of a battering ram, whose task it was to break the hard shell of a strong and powerful social system extending all over the world, needed to be as hard as diamond. The Revolution had to renounce tolerance, because nobody displayed tolerance in face of the "intrusion" of the proletariat, for the first time in history, at the head

54

of a state. It had to be hard and ruthless, although no more so than the first bourgeois revolution had been and, furthermore, much less so than the reactionary classes, throughout the centuries, have shown and continue to show themselves to be when in power.

In 1919, at one of the most crucial moments of the struggle, Lenin showed that *if the proletarian dictatorship found itself obliged to deny the bourgeoisie political freedoms, this was a special feature of the forms which that dictatorship took in Russia, and not a specific general characteristic of the system of transition from capitalism to socialism,* universal in its nature and validity. At the Eighth Congress of the Communist Party of the Soviet Union, in 1919, the founder of the Soviet state declared :

"We do not at all regard the question of disfranchising the bourgeoisie from an absolute point of view, because it is theoretically quite conceivable that the dictatorship of the proletariat may suppress the bourgeoisie at every step without disfranchising them. This is theoretically quite conceivable. Nor do we propose our Constitution as a model for other countries.

". . . while it is essential to suppress the bourgeoisie as a class, it is not essential to deprive them of suffrage and of equality."—(Collected Works, Vol. 29, pp. 184-5.) (My italics.—S.C.)

Lenin had already expressed this conception in one of the most famous of his polemical works, *The Proletarian Revolution and the Renegade Kautsky,* published in 1918 :

"It should be observed that the question of depriving the exploiters of the franchise is a *purely Russian* question, and not a question of the dictatorship of the proletariat in general.

". . . it would be a mistake . . . to guarantee in advance that the impending revolutions in Europe will all—or the majority of them—be necessarily accompanied by a restriction of the franchise for the bourgeoisie." (Collected Works, Vol. 28, p. 256.)

It is now clear that in the sphere of doctrine, Marxism-Leninism *not only fails to rule out, but actually foresees plurality of parties, political liberties and the possibility, furthermore, that a bourgeois opposition, too, may express itself electorally*, within the framework of the socialist revolution and the dictatorship of the proletariat. One must know how to separate the aspects of the socialist revolution that are *purely Russian*—as Lenin says—from the essential and universal content of that revolution, in working out our own line of march.

This is the Marxist-Leninist theoretical basis of our present socialist outlook.

The "Prague Coup"

In face of this our adversaries argue : "Good, we accept what is specific about the example of the U.S.S.R. But how, then, are we to explain the fact that the people's democracies in Eastern Europe, have been approaching the one-party system, and how are we to explain the 'Prague coup' [of 1948]?" The "Prague coup" crops up again and again, like a refrain, in all the accusations of totalitarianism that are made against our party. And it must be recognised that not a few of our own friends also have doubts about this matter. Perhaps we have not done all that we should have done to clarify this question. The truth is that often we make the mistake of thinking that what is clear to us is also clear to everyone else. Moreover we regard ourselves as satisfied and do not bother, as a rule, with explanations when an event results in a communist victory. Perhaps we ought to concern ourselves more in such cases with ensuring that our possible allies also understand the why and the wherefore of very important events.

At the time when they emerged, the people's democracies —all of them—were multi-party states. By the side of the Communist Party there were social-democratic and bourgeois parties which had a real existence and a great deal of vitality. Coalitions embracing various ones among

56

those parties were governing these countries and had carried out far-reaching economic reforms, in agriculture, industry, finance and commerce. These reforms had been favoured by the fact that in its advance towards Berlin the Soviet Army, on defeating the fascist troops, had decisively broken the structures of the reactionary states, making it objectively easier for the revolutionary forces which headed the national resistance movements, to carry out profound transformations. The people's democracies had already gone beyond the limits of the classical capitalist system, without as yet being completely socialist systems. As regards their content, they were anti-feudal and anti-monopolist democracies in which decisive sections of the economy had been nationalised. In 1947 and 1948 this process of development was disturbed; completely new problems and developments arose.

What had happened? Undoubtedly in that new situation an influence was exerted—how could it have been otherwise? —by the dispossessed sections of the big capitalists and landowners, a certain reaction on the part of the bourgeoisie as a class, which was sharpening the political situation within the coalitions established after the war.

There was, however, one fundamental factor which resulted in that reaction on the part of the old ruling classes and the bourgeois strata going to extremes—a factor without which matters would not have reached crisis point. That factor was *the cold war*. In 1947 the policy of imperialism— and especially American imperialism—was directed towards a rupture of the anti-Hitler coalition and towards the preparation of war against the Soviet Union, which was presented as being inevitable. The theory of *refoulement*, of winning back for capitalism the people's democracies in Europe, provided fresh encouragement for the remnants of the capitalist class in those countries and inspired them with a new combativeness. An important section of the leaders of the social-democratic and bourgeois parties began to see the prospect of a future hostile to socialism. Until then they had seen the prospect of socialism as something unavoidable, had adapted themselves to it and, with limitations and reservations, had collaborated. When the cold war began, a section of those leaders, directly encouraged and inspired by western embassies and services, changed course and took to the path of struggle for the restoration of capitalism.

United States imperialism, backed by the other imperialist powers and by the Second International and the Vatican, was at that time the by no means invisible orchestral conductor of a profound change in policy affecting the whole of Europe.

Those who talk about the "Prague coup" forget the prologue which that event had in capitalist countries of Europe, where before this there had been anti-communist "coups" supported by the might of the American forces of occupation and by the bourgeois state machines which had already been rebuilt. In France, Italy, Belgium and other countries the communists were expelled, *en bloc*, from the respective governments. In Western Germany the "coup" went so far as to outlaw the communists. In the fascist and reactionary countries—Spain, Portugal and Greece—the persecution of communists was intensified. A real anti-communist offensive was launched, preparing the conditions for military aggression.

Then, at the beginning of 1948, the U.S. imperialists and their satellites attempted to do in Prague what they had done in Paris, Rome and Brussels. At that point the communists, who were the strongest party electorally in Czechoslovakia, had no hostile intentions towards the other parties. Klement Gottwald, the President of the Czechoslovak Communist Party, told an American magazine in December 1947 that even if the Party gained an absolute majority in the forthcoming elections it would continue to maintain the multi-party system of government which then existed in his country.

In Czechoslovakia, the communists could not be so easily

58

kicked out of the Government as they had been in Paris and Rome; although American troops were still occupying Pilsen, the state apparatus had been reconstructed not on the basis of the old capitalist one but by the bringing together of all those who had taken part in the resistance, communists and non-communists; the workers had been organised in armed militia ever since the struggle against the German invader; in addition, the head of the Government was a communist and could not be expected to do what Ramadier had done in Paris—expel the Communist Ministers by decree.

Inspired by the United States and other western Embassies, President Beneš concocted a different plan, in agreement with the right-wing leaders of the bourgeois and socialist parties. It was, that the bourgeois and socialist Ministers should resign, bringing about a crisis which would give Beneš the opportunity to name a new head of Government and eliminate the communists. The socialist and bourgeois Ministers did resign. But the head of Government refused to do so, and solved the crisis by replacing them with other Ministers from their own parties. Meanwhile, within the Socialist Party and the bourgeois parties a real revolt had taken place against the right-wing leaders; new ones, men of the left and from the rank and file membership, who were against the restoration of capitalism and anti-Soviet collaboration with the western powers (those that had betrayed Czechoslovakia at the time of Munich and handed her over to Hitler) had taken over the leadership of these parties. The bourgeois and socialist leaders implicated in the plot were isolated. They then tried to turn back, withdraw their resignations and await a more favourable time for their coup. This was not acceptable either to the Government, to their own parties, or to the people and the workers, who came out on the streets in huge demonstrations demanding the expulsion of those who had resigned.

So a new Government was formed, consisting of communists, left-wing Social Democrats (who decided as a result

59

of these events to merge with the Communist Party) and left leaders of the bourgeois parties, which expelled their right-wingers and continued to function legally.

It can thus be seen that *what imperialist propaganda described as the "Communist coup" in Prague was nothing more than the defeat in Prague of the anti-communist coup that had succeeded in Rome and Paris.*

With their electoral majority in the country, assured of the support of the left socialist forces, the Catholics and the National Socialists (the party founded by Masaryk and Beneš), and with a majority in parliament, it was not the communists who attempted to carry out a coup d'état; they did not step outside constitutional legality. It was the right-wing conspirators, in line with imperialist manoeuvres. No party, in any country, would have allowed itself to be driven from power in such circumstances!

There is no doubt that these and similar events which took place in the People's Democracies and the capitalist countries, together with the stepping-up of the "Cold War", influenced the internal development of the new-type democratic States in eastern Europe, just as in the opposite sense they influenced the capitalist countries.

Preparations were made for military aggression against the socialist States, and they were obliged to prepare their defence. A sharpening of the class struggle ensued as a result. The dispossessed classes, encouraged by imperialist propaganda that promised the arrival of troops from the "Free World" to re-establish capitalist domination, adopted a more aggressive stance.

The conditions for collaboration with the bourgeois parties altered. The need for self-defence led to some reduction of the role of these parties. Nevertheless, in such countries as Poland, the German Democratic Republic and Czechoslovakia, they did not disappear, and are still represented in parliament and government.

What actually took place, therefore, in the People's Democracies was that the attitude of imperialism and the right wing of the bourgeois parties destroyed the previous political equilibrium. And in this way a transition which might have taken longer, with no restriction of liberty for the bourgeois groups, was speeded up and accompanied by certain restrictions which, despite all, cannot be compared with those that were forced upon the Russian revolution.

As international tension has relaxed, the non-communist parties in Poland and the German Democratic Republic have found their scope for action increasing.

In the Soviet Union, with the consolidation of the socialist system and the overcoming of the deviation of the "cult of the personality", the previous restrictions on freedom are disappearing. But this does not yet go far enough either for our opponents or for some of our friends. Because it is not accompanied by the legalisation and reappearance of the old bourgeois parties, either in their old forms or new ones. The restoration of political liberties in a country where antagonistic, exploiting and exploited classes have disappeared, assumes a quite different form from that which the same process might take in a capitalist country.

In Spain, for example, thirty years of dictatorship by a single fascist party are now coming to a crisis, one of the most remarkable features of which is the existence of a broad multi-party pluralism. We not only have the resurgence of such parties as the Communist, the Socialist, the Basque, Catalan and Galician nationalists, which existed before; various new groups are arising, democratic and liberal, several of them of Catholic origin, while the single party itself is splitting into different groups—the Monarchists, the Requetes, the Falangists, the Catholics. . . .

What is the reason for this proliferation of parties? The reason is that the dictatorship of the financial and land-owning oligarchy is working to the detriment of the other classes but it does not put them out of existence, does not abolish them, since the dictatorship cannot carry on without preserving and even developing the proletariat, without a peasant class, a non-monopoly bourgeoisie, or middle classes.

61

The fascist dictatorship cannot level and unify society; it is imposed by force and it exploits and impoverishes the whole of society, which continues to be divided into classes; it even accentuates the differences. When a crisis arises, the internal contradictions sharpen within the oligarchy itself which splits into wrangling groups.

The continuation and sharpening of class differences, and the division within the oligarchy, constitute the social foundation on the basis of which the recovery of political liberty coincides with—and expresses itself through—freedom for different political parties.

But in the Soviet Union—and this shows the vast difference between the nature of the proletarian and the bourgeois dictatorships—the dictatorship of the proletariat has brought about equality and unified society, wiping out the exploiting classes and all social privilege. In the Soviet Union the workers, the peasants and the intellectuals are friendly, socialist classes and strata. Objectively the disappearance of social antagonisms has meant the disappearance of the terrain in which political parties arise and grow. For this reason, the phenomenon of multi-party pluralism has disappeared naturally in the U.S.S.R. It is not that there are no longer any contradictions in Soviet society, but that these contradictions, which are not antagonistic, find expression through the whole variety of social organisations, the trade unions, the collective farm movement, the associations of women, youth and intellectuals. These contradictions do not affect the politico-social system; they do not express the desire of any class to dominate another. In future, when communism in its higher form becomes a reality, the Communist Party itself will disappear. Even today, the content of the work of the Communist Party in the U.S.S.R. is very different, because of the social transformations which have already taken place, from the content of that of the communist parties in the capitalist countries. This content is, essentially, socialist construction in the economy and in culture.

For reasons of space it is not possible to detail the forms which political freedom takes today in the U.S.S.R.; the advancement of the role of the Soviets and social organisations; the discussion of all important decisions by the broad masses; the selection from below of every candidate for public office before his or her candidature is made official in elections. It is evident that socialist democracy develops still further, starting, however, from premises conducive to the unification of society; while political democracy in the capitalist countries has to start from the opposite premise— the differentiation of society and the contrast between antagonistic classes.

The problem of the maintenance of multi-party pluralism and political freedom for the bourgeoisie in the period of transition from capitalism to socialism is bound up, as Lenin has taught us, with historical conditions, with the correlation of forces between one social system and another, with the attitude of the different parties and of the bourgeoisie.

The Role of the State in Society

The idea of the dictatorship of the proletariat as a stage in the transition from capitalism to communism rests on the Marxist concept of the role of the State. Marxists do not accept (and neither does life) the various bourgeois viewpoints which present the State as a force imposed from the outside of society, as an instrument of balance and judgment, beyond and above classes. Engels wrote :

"Because the state arose from the need to hold class antagonisms in check, but because it arose at the same time in the midst of the conflict of classes, it is as a rule the state of the most powerful, economically dominant class, and thus acquires new means of holding down and exploiting the oppressed class. . . . The state of antiquity was above all the state of the slave owners for the purpose of holding down the slaves, as the feudal state was the organ of the nobility for holding down the peasant serfs and bondsmen, and the modern representative state is an instrument of exploitation

63

of wage labour by capital." (*The Origin of the Family*, p. 168.)

This is to say, for Marxists, the different types and forms of state which have existed or do exist, including the representative or democratic state, are forms of domination by one class over others, *dictatorships* of certain classes against others. The idea of *dictatorship*, then, is fused with the idea of the state itself.

There appears to be a certain analogy here with anarchist concepts about the state. Nevertheless, the anarchists see the state as the personification of all evils and propose to destroy it overnight, while we Marxists regard the main evil as the existence of oppressed and oppressing classes. The state is no more than a consequence, an instrument. To put an end to capitalist society, the working-class and socialist forces need to possess, for a certain historical period, an instrument —their own state—to carry out this task. Only after the liquidation of capitalism on a world scale does the state lose its *raison d'etre* and wither away.

If we regard *dictatorship* as a form of state, this already enables us to draw a very important first conclusion : that the theoretical, scientific concepts (which is the sense in which we use the terms) of the *dictatorship of the proletariat* and the *dictatorship of the bourgeoisie* have little or nothing in common with the usual, current, most frequently used (even by us) meaning of the term *dictatorship*. This means that one can be at one and the same time opposed to it in the latter sense and in favour of what in theoretical terms is called *the dictatorship of the proletariat* or *the dictatorship of the bourgeoisie*. For example, bourgeois democrats, though they proclaim their opposition to "all dictatorships" and oppose fascist dictatorship, are in actual fact in favour of the dictatorship of the bourgeoisie in what one might call its "more benign" forms. At certain stages we can unite against *dictatorship*—in its usual, current sense, for example the Franco dictatorship or that of Salazar—with bourgeois and proletarian forces which are deeply divided on the question of the content of the state they want to bring about.

Of the two types of bourgeois state—i.e. of *dictatorship*—the proletariat unhesitatingly prefers the representative, democratic kind to the fascist kind.

From its very beginnings, democracy has been, at bottom, a form of dictatorship. In ancient Greece where the term was born, democracy was based on slavery. The 90,000 free citizens of Athens constituted a privileged class which exercised dictatorship over 360,000 *slaves who had no rights whatsoever*. In the same way in the Roman state (also a slave state) the people's assembly reflected a division into six classes on a property basis, and the top class—the richest—possessed the absolute majority in the assembly though it formed an insignificant minority in society. That is to say, the privileged minority in society exercised its dictatorship over the immense majority.

In the modern bourgeois democratic state, the minority of big capitalists exercise their dictatorship by more subtle though no less effective means. This minority controls the economic and political resources; the state apparatus is organised by it; the Army and the police are designed to protect the established order; the administration and the judicial system act in the same way. The laws are devised for the defence of big capitalist property. With economic and political power and the state apparatus in their hands, the big capitalists possess every variety of means of pressure to condition the behaviour of the great mass of apparently free voters. The radio, television, the mass-circulation press, the cinema, the theatre, publishing and advertising, all these —with some exceptions—are instruments which ideologically circumscribe the electorate and rob it of its independence. There is economic pressure, ranging from corruption to dismissal and blacklisting. And when this is not enough, there are the police and bourgeois justice, ready to intervene against the revolutionary forces.

Only in great revolutionary crises can the masses overcome their alienation and impose fundamental changes, including the transformation of the character of the state, a change of ruling class.

The example of Great Britain is typical. There they have a government elected by the working-class majority of which the population is composed. A government which calls itself socialist. Nevertheless, it has not modified one of the economic or state structures; instead it has frozen wages; its foreign policy servilely follows the lead of United States imperialism which holds it prisoner in the network of international finance, supporting the aggression in Vietnam. The present Labour government will pass away as the previous ones did; the capitalist system will remain intact. Labour M.P.s can be Ministers in the present state, but the working-class cannot win power. Thus this state, for all its political freedoms, does not cease to be a form of bourgeois dictatorship.

Capitalism dispenses with democratic methods when it finds itself in a weak position. It turns openly to fascist violence, abolishes political liberties, physically annihilates its opponents—even those of bourgeois persuasion. At this stage capitalist dictatorship takes on its most hateful, detestable form.

Petit-bourgeois and social-democratic critics of the *dictatorship of the proletariat* identify it with capitalist dictatorship in its fascist form, and have invented a common term for both : *totalitarianism*. This attempt to make a comparison between two completely opposite systems is an aberration which only serves capitalist interests.

We are fighting for a society from which the use of force by some men against others will be swept away, by a society without classes. While oppressed and oppressing classes exist, violence, under one form or another, will continue.

To declare oneself in principle against all violence, in a world in which imperialism and exploiting classes exist, to confuse the violence used by the exploiting classes condemned by history to preserve their privileges against other men—to confuse this with the violence which the oppressed

66

classes may be obliged to use against their oppressors; to confuse the violence of the oppressing imperialist powers with the violence of the peoples defending their freedom, leads willy-nilly to ranging oneself on the side of capitalism, the ultimate cause of all the violence in modern society. For instance, to put the violence of the U.S. invader, operating six thousand miles from his own country, on the same plane as the violence of the Vietnamese people, fighting on their own soil, defending their liberty inch by inch, is abject hypocrisy.

Yes! the dictatorship of the proletariat in Russia had to answer with violence the thousand times more brutal violence of the counter-revolution and the interventionists; it was forced, in order to subsist, to deprive its adversaries of political liberties and dissolve their parties. The People's Democracies, by much milder means and with far less violence, have had to restrict the bourgeois opposition and reduce the role of the non-communist parties in the conditions of the Cold War.

But between revolutionary violence and capitalist violence there are fundamental differences on which one must take a stand.

Fascist violence has the purpose of defending the privileges of the capitalist minority, to enlarge them at the cost of the misery and oppression of the great mass of the people.

Revolutionary violence puts an end to the privileges of the capitalist minority and gives possession of the social wealth to society, raising the standard of living, of culture, bringing about social equality.

Fascist violence leads to wars of aggression; it engenders aggressor states which provoke conflicts like the last world war.

Revolutionary violence engenders peaceful states which defend peace and co-existence and act as a barrier to the unleashing of new world wars.

Fascist, imperialist violence defends the most reactionary and discredited powers against their own peoples; it carries war and oppression beyond its own frontiers.

Revolutionary violence, and the states engendered by it, support those peoples who struggle against their oppressors, and oppose the forces of aggression and plunder.

Certainly, one of our objectives is to put an end to violence; but so long as there remain imperialists and capitalists who employ it, the oppressed and exploited who are its victims regard it as a sacred duty to resort to it for their own liberation.

Nevertheless, just as there was a vast difference between the violence that had to be employed by the Russian revolution and that which was necessary later on in the People's Democracies of eastern Europe, and just as there is a difference between the one-party system in the U.S.S.R. and the multi-party systems in some of the People's Democracies, the difference will be wider still when it comes to the socialist revolutions that in due course will take place in other European countries.

Political regimes, as a general rule, are the harsher as their basis of support is less strong nationally and internationally. Thus the possible forms of the dictatorship of the proletariat are bound up with the greater or lesser strength of the socialist system. In Russia, where socialism came into being in a situation of weakness, the forms were more violent. Today, socialism is much stronger. And those European countries which strike off the chains of imperialism and, in one way or another, achieve the revolution, will find support in the strength attained by the world socialist system. Starting off, furthermore, on an already-developed base of industrial and agricultural technique, not having to make the enormous effort at industrialisation that had to be made by the U.S.S.R. and other socialist countries which started off from a less advanced base, the new socialist states in Europe will quickly be able to give the mass of the people a higher living standard than their present one. The coercion necessary to abolish capitalism as a social class can be exercised within the framework of political democracy, without the need to deprive the members of the dispossessed classes of their political rights. It is possible that the younger members of these classes will sincerely give their support to socialism. In such conditions, the dictatorship of the proletariat will be a very different matter from the first dictatorship of the proletariat in the world. In Russia, at the beginning, the dictatorship of the proletariat was the dictatorship of a small minority of the population which sought support—not always easy to obtain—in an alliance with the peasants. In other countries, the dictatorship of the proletariat will be the government of the immense majority of wage-earners against a small minority who will not have to be deprived by the socialist revolution of their political rights.

The Broadening of Democracy
The main feature of the dictatorship of the proletariat is not, then, either the restriction of the political freedom of the class adversaries, or violence against the members of those classes. Its main feature is the step from capitalist ownership to social ownership; the transformation of the state, its organs and its laws, into a state which will undertake the task of carrying out and safeguarding the socialist transformation of society, the scientific organisation of production in the interests of the people, the development of culture and education, extending their benefits to the whole of society and putting an end to the class privilege which characterises it today; the moral formation of the new man.

In many countries of western Europe the progress towards socialism will probably take the form of a broadening of democracy, of the addition of a second dimension to political democracy—economic democracy. That is, government of the people, for the people and by the people—the formula for political democracy—together with the ownership by the people of the basic means of production and exchange and their utilisation by and for the people.

And this progress will probably go through a transitional

69

stage—anti-monopolist democracy—during which economic democracy will manifest itself by the nationalisation of the banks and the monopolies and consequently to the abolition of the monopolist oligarchy. In countries such as Spain it will be necessary at the same time to solve the question of the semi-feudal remnants in agriculture.

Even in these conditions, the victory of socialism will not come about as the result of a series of reforms in the heart of capitalist society. Of itself, anti-monopoly democracy will already effectively constitute a revolution, for it will demand a radical change of ownership and state power. The struggle for gradual reforms can contribute to the unification and bringing together of the forces capable of achieving this transformation. But only with the access to power of a democratic coalition strongly supported by the people, in which the working class has the leading position, able to impose the liquidation of the monopolist oligarchy, to break its ties—and those of its State—with international finance, and change the state apparatus so that it too becomes a firm support, only thus can this transformation be achieved. And this will be a genuine revolution.

This revolution can be carried out, in many instances, by democratic and peaceful means.

The theorists of neo-capitalism are always saying that there will be no revolution in the developed countries, that the communists will not succeed in rallying the majority of the people to carry it out, that class differences are fading away. But the truth is far otherwise. The truth is that the number of wage-earners is on the increase, even though a good number of them—as the means of production develop —may not be simple manual workers, but technicians and engineers. The truth is that the needs of the masses are rising as technical progress rises. And that in the modern industrial societies of Europe economic struggles are not decreasing; increasingly the technicians, professional people and various other working strata are taking part in them. The truth is that the attraction of Marxist ideology grows

70

ever greater, among the widest circles of society. The extreme concentration of ownership in the hands of State monopoly capital and the financial oligarchy; the contradiction between this oligarchy and the rest of society; the crises, which even if they have hitherto been less acute in character than before the Second World War, or even if they recur in different cycles, have not for this reason ceased to happen, and can become acute at any moment; the daily-deepening inter-imperialist contradictions; all the contradictions inherent in the capitalist system—all these will facilitate the task of rallying the working classes, raising their consciousness, and their militancy, and leading them to an ever more decisive struggle against the capitalist system.

The possibility of forming anti-monopoly coalitions of political and social forces, capable of attracting the majority of the population, will go on materialising, particularly as the present power groups in European countries exhaust themselves and reveal their inability to solve the present problems to the satisfaction of the mass of the people. In the present historical conditions, any shift towards the left, in countries where the communists are the essential force in this sector, could be the beginning of an evolution towards completely new political situations.

To sum up, the struggle for the victory of the anti-feudal, anti-monopoly and then the socialist revolution, will probably take the form of a struggle for the broadening of political democracy in this second economic dimension to which I have referred. We must repudiate, for this reason, all those accusations that imply that we are fighting for political liberties as a tactic so that we may suppress them later on. We must reject all tendencies to identify the forms which the socialist revolution may take in various European countries with those it took in Russia or elsewhere. This rejection by no means implies a lack of solidarity with the Russian revolution, for which we declare our full support. What is happening is that, largely due to the success of the

Russian revolution and those others which have preceded ours, ours will be able to assume very different forms.

The dictatorship of the proletariat will be a system of political democracy, multi-party. Power will be held by the great majority constituting the new army of wage-earners, together with vast forces of intellectuals; by the forces of labour and culture. The formula for this new form of the dictatorship of the proletariat will be, as we have stated : *government of the people, by the people and for the people; with the people owning the means of production, which will be administered by the people and for their benefit.*

THE ALLIANCE OF THE FORCES OF LABOUR AND CULTURE

In the conditions prevailing in our country, the struggle for political democracy is not directed to the replacement of one dictatorship by another; the course of the communists leads, on the contrary, to the constant strengthening of that democracy and its complementation by economic freedom. Already, in the course of the present struggles, the forces which can ensure the victory of political and economic democracy are taking shape and affirming themselves.

The leading class which is found at the head of these forces is the working class. The proletariat employed in industry, agriculture and the services comprises 63.7 per cent of the population. By means of tenacious and intelligent struggle the working people, the main victims of the Francoist victory, have won important economic gains from the dictatorial power of the oligarchy. But in addition, they have placed on the table the question of democratic freedom, starting off from the nearest available point : trade union freedom and the right to strike. Here the working class movement has not only formulated explicit demands, an important step forward in its time; with their unity and strength they have succeeded in imposing the use of the strike, of the mass demonstration and forms of organisation completely independent of capital and the Franco admini-

72

stration. All of what outside observers have called "the liberalisation of the regime" stems from these conquests which have not been ratified by any law but which are a fact. Effectively, these gains are changing the face of the Spanish political situation. It is they, and others which stem from the same basis, which have wiped out some of the most characteristically fascist features of the regime. We have said over and over again that the phenomenon of "liberalisation" is actually the retreat, the cornering of the regime as a result of the pressure and the advance of the democratic forces.

The resolute action of the working people has given rise to the new workers' movement, the Workers' Commissions, recognised by the most diverse political elements and by foreign correspondents the most remarkable politico-social event which has occurred in Spain in recent times. The Workers' Commissions hold the centre of public opinion today. Everyone seeks contact with them. Even those who oppose them are forced to recognise their existence, and attempt to influence them. The Private Secretary of the "Caudillo" (Franco) has himself entered into correspondence with those whom today they try to label "illicit associations". The Commissions are today the effective interlocutor for whoever seeks, with one object or another, to get in touch with the working class.

It is not impossible that the persecution of the Commissions may continue for a period and even momentarily sharpen; but the Commissions are already an indestructible reality. From whatever arbitrary procedure they are subjected to, they will in the long run emerge stronger. Persecution will mean that they will spread more widely and deeply. Still more will they become a weapon of defence and struggle for the mass of the workers. The *ultras* and the top hierarchy of the vertical syndicates* with their hatred for the Commissions and their repressive measures, will only achieve, in spite of themselves, the opposite result from what they want : their strengthening and consolidation.

* The state-controlled "trade unions" of the Franco regime.

The Workers' Commissions have adopted the forms that were available to them in the circumstances; nevertheless, they are by no means creatures of circumstance. With intelligence and foresight they have charted a course for the future which shows their fitness to become permanent and play an essential part in the political and social life of Spain.

Their programme makes clear that the working class intends to assume the leading role in the struggle for political and economic democracy in Spain, not forgetting their international duty and the contribution which circumstances may enable them to make to the cause of the unity of the workers of the whole world.

In this programme the working class proclaims its national character, taking over and incorporating with their demands the demands of the peasant masses, the students and intellectuals and the anti-monopoly groups—in a word, the broad democratic sections of the whole country.

Alongside the Workers' Commissions are springing up new, independent forms of unity and struggle by other anti-Franco classes and strata.

The peasant movement, taking ever more heed of the forms of organisation and struggle of the proletariat, is growing. The peasants are organising *strikes*—the milk strike, the resin strike; they are forming co-operatives—signs of growth of the collectivist trend originating from the workers; they are creating independent Commissions and associations; they are starting to combine legal forms—a series of Brotherhoods—with extra-legal ones. The contact between workers and peasants is growing at local and provincial levels. The alliance between the city workers and those of the countryside will come about in this way. It can be foreseen that gradually, this whole process of independent organisation by the peasants and alliance with the working class will reach new heights, rising in the course of the struggle and the overcoming of the difficulties and obstacles that stand in the way of their advance.

In the student sector we find a powerful, independent,

democratic movement that has wrecked the SEU and its offspring the AP* and imposed a new Union, created by the masses in the struggle against the Francoist structures. The student movement is a progressive force of great value and significance. By its struggle and its objectives it is moving into the deep national current that is pressing for political and economic democracy, for the type of University it demands is barely conceivable in a political and economic system dominated by the finance and landowning oligarchy. Furthermore, its solidarity w⁺th the working class, its resolute actions in support of the workers' struggles, its efforts towards co-ordination, reveal the deep movement for renovation that inspires it.

A growing part of the teaching staff supports the students, adopts ever more committed positions, joins in the struggle.

Broad sections of the intellectuals are following a progressive line which has not been retracted during recent years, which we have mentioned earlier in this work. This has been very recently shown by the new declarations in support of the arrested workers' leaders and the Workers' Commissions movement. There has never been a document in Spain signed by so many professors, writers, artists in support of specifically working-class demands—minimum wage, sliding scale, trade union freedom, the right to strike—as the one recently published with 565 of their signatures. This is the sign of a new attitude on the part of the mass of the intellectuals towards the working class movement, an attitude full of promise for future collaboration. But all this activity shows the existence of a certain link-up among the intellectuals themselves, by means of multiple and various contacts, with a definite degree of unity and organisation, still somewhat loose but moving towards concrete and effective forms.

The same trend is becoming apparent among a considerable number of different specialists—engineers, architects,

* *Sindicato Español Universitario*, a compulsory student union; *Asociaciones Profesionales*, a similar organisation which succeeded the first upon its collapse.

technicians and administrative personnel—who in some enterprises are actively collaborating with the workers' movement, becoming conscious of their position as wage-earners, recognising the identity between their interests and those of the rest of the working people. Associations and other kinds of democratic groups have been formed, which are tending to link up with the Commissions.

Very important moves have recently taken place among the medical profession. An organised movement is arising in defence of the more-than-jus·ified demands of a profession as essential as it is neglected, demands not only economic in character, but also political and moral. An example is the opposition to the new system of regulations for the Medical Colleges, drawn up on the basis of a police mentality in the office of Don Camilo Alonso*; this is an opposition which basically brings the doctors, who are standing up for freedom and democracy as the working regulations for their Colleges, into the same sphere of action as that of the workers and students who are defending their right to form their own unions.

It can be expected that other professional groups will adopt similar positions. The intellectuals will thus become integrated, in their most varied sections and through many different channels with the movement for democratic renewal that is stirring Spanish society to its very depths.

Part of this, and a very important part, is the profound conciliary prophetic and progressive current, which is making itself felt in the Spanish Church and the Catholic movement, and is one of the most dynamic wings of present social development. This current has been shown to possess effective co-ordination in a number of cases, notably on the occasion of the so-called "Operation Moses".

* Alonso Vega, Camilo, retired as Lieutenant-General in 1955; Minister of the Interior from 1956 to 1969. Left Cabinet in major reorganisation of October 1969 at the age of 80. On leaving the government he was promoted to the rank of Captain-General, a rank held only by two other Spaniards, General Franco and General Augustin Muñoz Grandes.

Forms of organisation are also beginning to appear among the small proprietors adversely affected by the dictatorship of the monopolist oligarchy. It is hoped that these forms, like others embracing artisans and small businessmen, will develop further in the future.

A characteristic feature of the present situation are the multifarious ties existing between all these movements, which tend to bring them increasingly into a single front of action. The Workers' Commissions, the peasant opposition, the student union, the various intellectual and professional groups and the above-mentioned Catholic sectors are not strangers to one another; they are linked by ties which are frequently informal but are nevertheless effective. This connection springs from a natural, spontaneous tendency, whose origin is the community of interests and objectives. No repression, no coercion will be able to halt this natural tendency, which is leading to forms of organisation ever more conscious and articulated, that will very probably manifest themselves in due course in an open and declared manner.

What, essentially, is all this movement, of a breadth and character unknown in the past?

Essentially it means the upsurge of an alliance of the broadest forces of Labour and Culture, an event which must be welcomed with exhilaration.

The alliance of the forces of Labour and Culture— workers and office employees, peasants, creative intellectuals, scientists and professional people, artists, students, artisans, small manufacturers and businessmen—is taking its first steps. It will have to confront serious trials and difficult obstacles in order to solidify and affirm itself fully. It is still too soon to try and foresee the forms it will eventually take.

But it is evident that the alliance, headed by the working class and its Commissions, is already a real force which is beginning to cause a crisis in the Fascist political structure, to lay the basis of Spain's future democracy, gaining ground step by step through action and struggle. This movement is the most real and effective force which the dictatorship is up against.

It is also characteristic that this alliance is not coming about as a result of an agreement between political parties, as other alliances did in former times. It is being formed from organisations which have a social base. This is an indication, in our opinion, that in Spain's future democracy the social formations are likely to play a much greater role than in other periods.

This in no way signifies that the alliance expresses the existence of any lack of political feeling among the mass of the people, as I have already shown earlier. In action within the various mass movements are not a few people who are connected with different political parties or groups. What is plainly shown by these special characteristics of the alliance of the forces of Labour and Culture is, on the contrary, the widespread *politicalisation* of the masses, which is also extending to vast sections that have not hitherto aligned themselves with any particular party or group.

It can also be gathered from the foregoing that the mass movement towards alliance is running ahead of, outstripping, the attitude of certain groups and parties which resist unity—which is a proof of the political maturity of the masses.

Nevertheless, this alliance, which is taking shape among the most varied democratic social movements, is having some influence on the attitude of the political parties. Thanks to it, a closer approach is taking place among them, though it is still insufficient. This closer approach is causing something of a crisis among the leaderships, a crisis that arises precisely from the fact that the leaders, in many cases, did not reckon that the masses could play the active part which they are playing in the struggle, and based their strategy on combinations arrived at from above, making them dependent on conflicts which might arise inside the leading groups. Some of these leaders must now face the problem of a change of direction which is not always easy for them to carry out.

However, it can be expected that as the *alliance of the forces of Labour and Culture* develops, the democratic political groups will seek ways to become part of it, alongside the organised movements of the working class and other sections of society.

In any case, it is already clear that the *alliance of the forces of Labour and Culture*, when it attains fuller development and definitive forms, will not be simply an alliance of parties, but a mixed alliance of social organisations and parties.

It is not possible to outline a fixed scheme for the future. But a likely prospect, which we should grasp, is that the *alliance of the forces of Labour and Culture* will in future become the great politico-social formation which, once political democracy has been attained, will undertake the task of complementing it by the realisation of economic, anti-feudal and anti-monopoly democracy.

In the future the alliance could set itself the aim of taking power, by democratic means, with the active support of the mass struggle, so as to accomplish the historic task of broadening political democracy with economic democracy.

Later on, after a prolonged period of transition, when Spain would have succeeded in providing herself with modern means of production, profiting from the achievements of the present scientific and technical revolution, the alliance itself might be the body called on to proceed from this anti-monopolist, anti-feudal democracy to the establishment of the socialist system.

In that event, *the power which would ensure the transition from capitalism to socialism would be a power of the alliance of the forces of Labour and Culture*, a democratic, multi-party power.

This system of transition would be very different in form from what has occurred in other countries, though it would carry out the same fundamental task which was performed in those countries by the *dictatorship of the proletariat* : the transformation of private ownership into collective owner-

79

ship, the organisation of a socialist State.

A group of Catholic workers, the AST,* in its programme has explained its conception of the role of the State in these terms :

"We understand the State.

"As an indispensable organ, *under the control* of the people, playing a role of extraordinary importance in the stage which exists from the commencement of the revolution to the full realisation of genuine socialist society. . . .

"The task of the state is : the overall planning of the economy, in direct relation with the organised working-class forces. The protection of the different national groups, within the community. The promotion of culture at all levels, being careful to see that there is genuine equality of opportunity for access to it. The protection of the different ideological tendencies, while always safeguarding the integrity of the revolution. The fostering of a change of outlook, which should prevent the revolution from becoming a mere change of structures, making its mainstay the transformation of man. It should also encourage and protect the formation and development of all groups or institutions which the people may need for their total advancement."

The State of transition from capitalism to socialism which we communists want in the condition of Spain, does not greatly differ from what AST upholds in these lines.

The alliance of the forces of Labour and Culture would be the body which would wield this power.

In formulating this perspective and declaring for it, we communists have in mind a problem which exists, in very similar terms, for almost all our brother parties in the countries of western Europe, which each faces up to and tries to solve according to the specific situation in its country, its own historical experience and, of course, the lessons of the great Soviet and other revolutions. It is a question of the character, the social composition and the forms of the

* See page 36.

alliance of forces required for proceeding to the socialist revolution.

The Communist Party is the Marxist-Leninist vanguard; but even in those countries where it is numerically strongest, the Communist Party does not—and neither does it seek to —include the whole of the working class in its ranks, still less all the classes and social strata which at a certain juncture may lean towards socialism.

Other parties and tendencies also organise sections of the workers and the people. In many countries the Socialist Party is a force of considerable importance among the working people.

Without unity between the communists and these sections and the parties that represent them, how can the march towards socialism be conceived?

In Russia, the worker-peasant alliance was and is the basis of the revolution and of socialist power. In other countries, ours included, this alliance is also an important factor.

But in our country—and even more so in other western countries more developed than ours—the ratio between proletariat, peasantry and other middle strata is not the same as that which existed in the old Russia, where the proletariat was a small minority in the midst of an ocean of individual peasant producers.

In our country the alliance needed for victory must also have in mind the urban middle strata and must strive at all costs to win a part of them over. The problem is how to devise a policy which will also influence these sections and mobilise them with us against monopoly capital and—in Spain—against the remnants of feudalism.

The question of the form of the alliance is very important. An alliance, or a single party uniting all the socialist and progressive forces?

For our country, on the basis of our experience, we communists do not regard a single party for all the socialist and progressive forces as useful or even possible.

81

On the one hand, if we were to attempt this, we should have the old charge of "absorptionism" levelled against us —the intention to move on to a *single party* system and "liquidate" the other parties. In effect, a single party on the basis of Marxism-Leninism would be a communist party.

On the other hand, what would a single party be without a common ideological basis, without class homogeneity? It would be the scene for a constant clash of different fractions, social classes and schools of thought which would paralyse its action and deprive it of revolutionary capacity.

An alliance, the forms of which can evolve and be adapted according to need, is the formula which will permit the co-existence in one body of various parties and organisations, of different schools of thought, each retaining its personality and independence, having the right to put forward its solutions to each problem and carry on its own propaganda. At the same time, the common zone of aims and decisions could be sustained by a common discipline for their achievement and by common political organisations to apply them and carry them out.

Such an alliance could become very solid, very well-articulated, very coherent in pursuing the common policy and aims, without any organisation or party feeling itself diminished.

This is the prospect opened up by the new Spanish workers' movement and the various other mass movements which are moving in the same direction today. It depends on us and on the progressive elements whether this possibility is transformed into a reality.

THE POSITION OF THE COMMUNIST PARTY

How do we conceive the position of the Communist Party within the alliance of the forces of Labour and Culture? Not as a specially privileged position, but as having the same rights and duties as the other parties and organisations which go to make it up. This can be inferred from the multi-party and democratic character which we envisage for the entire road towards democracy and socialism. This does not mean that we renounce the leading role of the Marxist-Leninist party of the proletariat; it means that the exercise of this role should be adapted to the forms which the transition to socialism will take in our country.

In the basic experience gained up to now, characterised—with exceptions—by the existence of the Communist Party as the only party, the party has had to make within itself a synthesis of the various opinions which arise in society with regard to the solution of problems. Decision comes from the party already taken, at any rate on the really important questions and at times on less important ones. The role of the vanguard in this instance is to *define and apply* the solutions.

In a multi-party system, the leading role of the Communist Party does not consist in making the synthesis, finally, by itself. It consists in proposing the solutions it considers appropriate or raising its objections to the proposals of other parties or groups, and then contributing to the working out of a synthesis jointly with them. The work of synthesis, of arriving at a solution, is carried out, then, not inside the Party but within the democratic institutions, with the participation of all the socialist forces. And its application is not the responsibility of the organs of the Party but that of the institutions of the State.

In this situation, the Party continues to play its *leading role, but not a dominant role.** The dominant role belongs

* Author's footnote: The use of the word *dominant* may give rise to confusion if one is not warned that what I am trying to convey is simply the difference between the position of a Party which holds power without sharing it with others, which thereby *dominates* the entire leadership of the State, and the position of the same Party sharing power with others and exercising a leading role solely as a consequence of its better preparation for the historical tasks of the State of the transition and not because it possesses all the instruments of power. Actually this is a new practical problem, which explains the difficulty of finding an adequate term in current Marxist terminology.

83

to the working class and the whole of the alliance which is in power.

The Party exercises its leading role to the extent that it brings together in its ranks the vanguard elements of the proletariat and other working classes and strata; that it is able to apply Marxist-Leninist methods in analysing situations and formulating its programme and proposals; that it possesses a precise understanding of reality and goes deeply into the knowledge of possibilities and necessities; that it is an active, homogeneous and disciplined whole, able to swing its entire weight and influence in any direction necessary; that its members set an example of ability, honesty, self-sacrifice and the spirit of service in the interests of the people. The Party exercises its leading role to the degree that it is able, by its correct policy, its combined flexibility and firmness, to maintain and consolidate the alliance, isolating and politically combating the foes of the alliance.

The Party does not impose its decisions on others; it persuades, convinces, and accepts the reasonable modifications proposed by its allies. The imposition or application of collective decisions, when they are finally reached, is done by the State organs charged with such work. At the same time, this system means that it is not always the Party which takes the initiative in arriving at solutions; the initiative in various instances can come from others. It means that a proposal by the Party can be rejected and the Party must yield to democratic decision, which does not prevent it, if it thinks fit, from raising this proposal again, if it was a correct one, on another occasion when experience has convinced its allies and they have come to understand the need for it. That is to say, that in a system of this nature, the contradictions which can arise between friendly strata and classes engaged in a common undertaking must be solved by methods of persuasion and conviction, relying on practical experience.

The composition of the Government and the State organs of power must be made up on the basis of this plurality and of actual capacities and merits, among which ability and honesty should be the most highly valued. This means that during the stage of transition from capitalism to socialism the Party can have more or fewer Ministries, more or fewer leading positions in the Government, without this being the most significant barometer of its leading role, which will depend, in the last resort, above all on its ties with the masses and its ability to mobilise them.

In that period it will be necessary to reckon with the resistance and activity of the hostile dispossessed classes and their remnants, who will be more or less dangerous according to whether or not imperialism is in a position to rely on them and utilise them against the new regime. So long as these remnants stay within the framework of legality and show themselves without concealing their nature and their programme, they ought not to be deprived of their political rights. But it will be necessary to remain extremely vigilant with regard to attempts by these elements to infiltrate into the parties and organisations of the alliance for the purpose of stirring up conflicts and friction among them, and using them as a cover for counter-revolutionary activity. Democracy does not mean weakness or laxity in face of actions whose purpose is to subvert the new social order.

In a State of transition with these forms, the leading role is exercised both by participation in leadership and decision-making and by criticism of both these in cases where they are not correct. The Party is concerned to safeguard the freedom to criticise, within the framework of friendship and collaboration, the actions of its allies and also those of its own representatives when they make mistakes in carrying out their tasks. The Party has no reason to assume or seem to assume responsibility for the administrative decisions of any government organ; it will approve and support them or criticise them according to whether they are correct or no.

This conception does not presuppose any weakening of the leading role of the Party; it supposes an adaptation of this role to the forms which the present level of historical

85

development may allot to the stage of transition from capitalism to socialism in our country. It is obviously impossible to conceive of a multi-party system in which the formal status of our Party would be different from and privileged above that of other parties. The leading role will not be guaranteed by any legal formality or special treatment; it will be ensured by the political and ideological ability and the mass strength of the Party, in a natural way.

Here lies the difference between a Party which both *leads and dominates*—the latter because historical circumstances necessitated the apparent merging of these two features due to the tremendous resistance which internal and external counter-revolution was in a position to put up—and a Party which exercises its *leading* role in the framework of a dominant coalition established in power.

In outlining and establishing this prospect, we are not acting in any spirit of manoeuvring, to try and "bamboozle" our possible allies and reduce the resistance to our advance. We fully understand that the Communists of the Soviet Union and other countries have had to adopt other methods for the march towards socialism. At one time Lenin thought that in Russia, too, multi-party forms could be used which would not deprive bourgeois groups of their rights. It is significant that Lenin believed in this possibility at the time when he was also looking forward to the prospect of an imminent victory for the revolution in Europe; that is to say, he linked this possibility with the strength which the socialist revolution could have possessed had it triumphed in the most developed continent. This position of strength for the revolution did not, unfortunately, come about then, but it is beginning to do so today, and becoming once again a present possibility which, though it faded away in Russia when the revolution was confined to a single country, continued to be envisaged by Lenin for other countries when he referred to the variety of political forms of future revolutions and to what was *specifically* Russian in the Soviet experience.

For this reason, when we favour these forms we do so not because we disapprove of, or lack solidarity with, those which had to be adopted by the socialist revolutions in other countries. It is precisely because these were made by such methods and forms as were possible in their circumstances, that the new ones will be able to vary their paths and use different forms. One and all will be inspired by Marxism-Leninism, for there is no other consistently revolutionary doctrine but this.

The new forms which the revolution may take do not, I repeat, mean any diminution of the Party's leading role; they simply mean a new form of this role. A new form which makes it just as essential, if not more so, that the Communist Party should be strong both in quality and number; in its ability and mass support; in its political and ideological staunchness and its audacity; in its cohesion and its democratic internal life. Democracy and socialism in Spain require a great Communist Party.

A Mass Communist Party

The organisation of a mass Communist Party is already one of today's tasks. It is a task which must be conceived as a development, with various forms, not always cut and dried or "classical", but in transition. If, in a situation like that of today, we were to attempt to organise the *entire* membership, *all* the Communists, in factory or local cells or local rural organisations strictly supervised from top to bottom by the leading bodies; if we were to require *all* the Communists regularly to fulfil their obligations to meet, take part in the work of a basic Party organisation and pay their dues in that organisation, we should be banging our heads against the brick wall of reality. The reality is, that in a situation of dictatorship which retains many of its fascist features, a Party like ours, a Marxist-Leninist Party, in order to be a mass Party, must combine regular, classical forms, which group together the most developed and most experienced members for the illegal struggle, with irregular, looser

87

and less strict forms of organisation, formally less exacting and less hazardous but not thereby less effective in a period such as we are living in.

What are these forms? How shall we hit on them? In this respect nothing needs to be invented; the masses will invent for us, and what remains to be done is to study what the masses invent, develop it, draw conclusions from it, and rely firmly on it, without lumbering ourselves with doctrinal formulas which are correct enough but which apply to *stable* situations of one kind or another and not to situations of transition and upheaval such as we are experiencing.

On this kind of question, let us go back to Lenin, in whose works, so varied and so rich, are to be found the most profitable lessons a proletarian revolutionary can use. In speaking of a Leninist party we are accustomed to refer to three conditions of membership : accept the Party's pro-gramme, work in a Party organisation; and pay dues. But Lenin said something else about the Party in certain situations. He wrote :

"A revolutionary epoch is to the Social-Democrats* what war-time is to an army. We must broaden the cadres of our army, we must advance them from peace strength to war strength, we must mobilise the reservists, recall those on leave, and form new auxiliary corps, units and services. . . .

"To drop metaphor," (he added), "we must considerably increase the membership of all Party and Party-connected organisations in order to be able to keep up to some extent with the stream of popular revolutionary energy which has been strengthened a hundredfold."—(*New Tasks and New Forces*, Collected Works, Vol. 8, p. 211.)

And Lenin did not confine himself to repeating the formulas he had drawn up in *What is to be Done?* which continue, in general, to retain their validity; he had in mind the exceptional situation which the revolutionary movement

* At that time the separation between communists and social democrats had not taken place and the workers' party bore the name Social-Democratic.—S.C.

was in, and stated :

"If we stop helplessly at the achieved boundaries, forms and confines of the committees, groups, meetings and circles, we shall merely prove our own incapacity. Thousands of circles are now springing up everywhere without our aid, without any definite programme or aim, simply under the impact of events. The Social-Democrats must make it their task to establish and strengthen direct contacts with the greatest possible number of these circles, to assist them, to give them the benefit of their own knowledge and experience, to stimulate them with their own revolutionary initiative. Let all such circles, except those that are avowedly non-Social-Democrat, either directly join the Party or *align themselves with the Party*. In the latter event we must not demand that they accept our programme or that they necessarily enter into organisational relations with us. Their mood of protest and their sympathy for the cause of international revolutionary Social-Democracy in themselves suffice, provided the Social-Democrats work effectively among them, for these circles of *sympathisers* under the impact of events to be transformed at first into democratic assistants and then into convinced members of the Social-Democratic working-class party."—*New Tasks and New Forces*. Collected Works, Vol. 8, pp. 219, 220.

At the present moment, I repeat, we Spanish Communists need not to invent forms of organisation but to rely on those which are springing up in life itself, and extend them. We do not need to ask ourselves what to do to become a mass party; we need to ask *how we have become a mass party*, in order to find the way to continue our development in this direction.

If we have succeeded in becoming a mass party, this is due in the first place to the fact that we possess a mass policy, a policy which can be understood by the workers, the people and the youth; a policy which corresponds with the feelings and interests of the great mass of the people. In this connection, a curious attitude is shown by members of other groups who fail to respond to many of our initiatives or proposals because they happen to come from us and have not occurred to them first. If we could, we would form ourselves into an *"office for the creation of popular initiatives"*, to provide some for them.

In fact, without an understandable policy which reaches out to the masses, which the masses adopt and make their own, a mass party is impossible, either in our conditions or in more favourable ones.

The conclusion is clear : we must continue to develop a policy which interprets every day more accurately the interests and sentiments of the mass of the people.

The second thing that has enabled us to become a mass party is that we have established a system of regular organisations and committees—which still needs enlarging and strengthening—formed from the core of trained and experienced members who are able to bring our correct policy to the masses and organise their activity and struggle in the most varied forms and sections. It cannot be doubted that this system of organisations and committees forms the backbone of the party and that we must pay fundamental attention to its development, the constant strengthening of its composition, and the raising of the political and ideological levels of its activity. Together with this goes the need for ever greater efforts to promote and train new cadres from among young men and women.

The third factor is the attention paid to the mass movement, to the formulation of its problems, to its organisation —in the first place among the working class but also in the countryside, among the intellectuals and students, the women and the youth; the attention paid to all kinds of questions—industrial, economic, cultural, housing, public service, etc. It can be seen that in those provinces where the basic, stable leading core of the party organisation has shown the greatest ability to tackle all the broad range of questions which concern one section or another of the people, our strength has correspondingly increased.

Wherever we have paid better and more thorough attention to these problems the strength of the Party has grown considerably. Thousands of veteran communists who had become scattered by the fascist repression in previous periods have thrown off their passivity, or semi-passivity, and become active once again. Other thousands of new members have come to the fore, with great militancy and enthusiasm.

When we put forward the proposal in 1960 to drive towards a mass Party, our ability to mobilise the masses bore no comparison to that which we can show today. Only because we are a mass Party can we achieve what we are doing today, though it is clear that we still have much to do.

We have already succeeded in organising a proportion of these thousands of old and new members in regular units, built in a solid and stable way. Thus we can say without boasting that ours is one of the strongest Communist Parties in western Europe. But a further and still greater section of active communists—as active and sometimes more active than the regularly-organised ones—who follow our line and initiatives, support our programme and carry out effective Communist work among the masses, are not in the regular organisations. And this is so, not only because of defects in the work of this or that regular organisation but in most cases because of the real, objective difficulties which arise from the existence of the dictatorship. We must ask ourselves : where are these Communists? Through what channels do they receive the guidance of the Party? How, in what manner and in what conditions do they join together in action—which is to say, what political life do they have? What are, in actual fact, their links with the Party? And it is the serious answer to these questions, gained from a close study of reality, which will bring us clarity as to the various forms of organisation, non-classical, flexible and loose, in which we are already, in present circumstances, bringing together those members of the Party who are not integrated in the regular organisations. On the basis of this we shall be

91

able to see how to improve these forms of organisation, how to regularise them gradually, and also how to develop others of a similar kind.

Examination will show us that a great part of these communists are active in the new workers' movement, in social and cultural associations, in mass youth or women's activities, in many-purpose circles and recreational groups which are arising today on all sides as a result of the activation and growing political awareness of the broad masses. In these movements today, active political discussion goes on around national and often international political problems and, of course, about the concrete problems of the masses, not just among communists but among all those taking part in them. It is probably here that the most frequent and the most open discussion takes place. Though it may seem paradoxical, the political life of many of those comrades who are working in this type of movement is more active than that of some of the members who are organised in Party cells but do not take an active part in these movements.

When we investigate this question, we shall see that those Communists normally receive the Party's guidance through other comrades who work both in regular party organisations and in those various mass movements or groups and give active support to these latter. They also receive written propaganda fairly regularly. In many cases they assiduously follow the broadcasts of *Radio España Independiente*. The problem is to find formulas that will consolidate these political ties without the necessity, for the moment, of bringing all Communists into cells, which will certainly happen when the political situation opens up more than at present and excessive extension of the regular forms will not constitute a danger to the security of the Party itself.

But from now on we must regard these comrades as members of the Party, and keep their existence in mind when political activity is being planned. At present this does not always happen; they are looked on at most as sympathisers, regardless of the fact that in the great majority of cases their activity will stand full comparison with that of fully paid up members, and also that many of them contribute from time to time to Party funds.

This attitude towards them reveals the persistence of ideas left over from the period when the most tightly-maintained clandestinity was essential; today, these ideas are out of place, and in fact reveal an attitude of drawing back from and rejection of the new mass forces, an attitude which must be overcome.

The same reluctance is shown in the fact that the greater part of our organisations are without any recruiting policy. While other groups, so far as they are able, are actively engaged in the work of making converts—as can be testified by many of our comrades who have been asked to join them —the Party organisations do not seriously go out to win new members. Those who join the Party usually do so on their own initiative and after a difficult search; they have to knock at the door and almost kick it down. And nevertheless, each organisation today knows dozens of men and women who are outstanding for their attitude of protest, for their support for our ideas, for their defence of the Party in many instances, and for their militancy. It would only need some methodical work with these people for the majority of them to join the Party quite soon.

Although it is true that we are still underground, that we must be extremely careful to guard our apparatus and illegal organisation from police provocations and repressive attacks, it is no less true that we possess fresh possibilities and a very different situation from that of other periods.

Today, thousands of communists are known as such to the masses and to our adversaries, since they themselves do not conceal their ideas though they do conceal—naturally enough—their membership of the underground organisation. This means that the political work of the communists is now less clandestine; in certain cases it verges on semi-legality. It is correct to proceed in this way, because by taking this road the Party will blossom out into the open

93

and will one day achieve legality.

So long as the *ultras* continue to hold key positions in the Government, the danger of provocations and repressive measures remains. We cannot lose sight of this. But at the same time we must face the fact that the situation in general, and the position of the Communist Party in particular, have changed considerably. The Communist Party represents the most serious threat to the privileges of the ruling classes and the toughest adversary of the dictatorship. But bourgeois propaganda, our political opponents, are now no longer of one mind—as they were in the period of the cold war and before—as to the methods to use against the communists. Those who think that the "communist problem" can be reduced to a matter of "public order" are becoming steadily fewer, though this continues to be the official attitude of the regime and some of its out-of-date defenders.

The near-collapse of the Franco dictatorship, the proximity of political change, means that various sections of the bourgeoisie are beginning to view the communist phenomenon more calmly.

In an article which dealt in a general way with Europe, the daily newspaper, *Madrid* acknowledged that in the Latin countries, where social tensions are acute, the existence of important Communist Parties must be admitted. And it added that, from the time when a Communist Party is able to win the votes of millions of people, it is preferable that it should act in legality than that it should be driven underground. Although the article made no direct reference to Spain, what reason could there be for applying to our indubitably Latin country a criterion different from that considered suitable for the others?

It is ever more usual to read press articles and commentaries which state that the way to weaken the influence of communism is to put an end to the abuses and social injustices which exist.

On the other hand, the turn towards the establishment of normal relations with the socialist countries provides the opportunity for the publication of reports and articles—some of them genuinely objective—on the progress attained in these countries, articles which can help—though not written with this purpose—to disarm the fierce and poisonous anti-communism which has been used to justify the particularly savage repression against our Party.

When my statements were published in *Le Figaro* and *L'Unità* the (Spanish) press, radio and television gave a lot of attention to the attitude of the Communist Party. To be sure, they did so on the basis of extracts transmitted by the EFE Agency, in which my remarks were shamelessly falsified with the aim of putting the Catholics "between the sword and the wall" on the one hand, and creating difficulties for the Workers' Commissions on the other. There was nothing in my statements which gave cause for any action against the Catholics, and even less against the Workers' Commissions. Furthermore, at that particular time, the regime, particularly the *ultras*, was more worried than ever before about the conciliar Catholics and the Workers' Commissions.

But what is interesting is the fact that although the comments published in the newspapers and periodicals of the "Movement"* stick to the lines laid down by the falsifications of the EFE and hurl the basest and most ridiculous charges against the communists, other newspapers comment on the statements in a different tone. And some have made no comment, perhaps refusing in this way to give credence to the falsifications.

Certainly, those journals whose comments differ in tone from those of the "Movement" do not support our viewpoint; they reject this or that aspect of it; nevertheless, some admit, as a matter of course, that the Catholics and the communists are jointly concerned with workers' rights. The difference is that in some cases they argue against us without slandering us and in some cases with a hitherto-unknown respect.

* The National Movement, the only legal party in Spain.

Whatever the repercussions of this treatment of us by the press and information media of the regime, the fact is that the widespread diffusion of the statements shows the real weight which the Communist Party has in present day Spain despite being illegal and persecuted.

In some of the Catholic periodicals, the change of attitude towards the Communist Party is more openly expressed. To mention only recent examples, I shall quote the questionnaire initiated by the Catholic youth magazine *Signo* among various members of the clergy. Two of the questions which were put turned on the *obligation* (or otherwise) to hold a dialogue or even collaborate with supporters of "scientific atheism" in the trade union sphere, for example, and whether a priest can be a friend "in the deepest sense of the word" with a Communist. The reply of Father José María de Llanos was decidedly positive. That of Father Marino Alvarez Mínguez of Almería stated :

"Collaboration with atheists in practice for the construction of the world is an obligation. It is a question of fostering of the Common Good which benefits us all. Individualism, the 'ghetto', are heresy in our times. Trade union collaboration, and collaboration in the broad social, economic, cultural and political field, are a necessity."

Father José Casco of Málaga, a former counsellor to the JOC, replied :

"I believe that the evangelical approach is to make no discrimination or condemnations of any kind. The dialogue should go on, without fear or false circumspection. In the trade union as in many other spheres we have a very long way to travel, in company with many men."

Lastly, Father José Maria González Ruiz expressed himself in these words :

"In any case the dialogue between believers and non-believers must be held, but it should take place in the context of the collaboration that both have to lend to the building of the world. Today, for example, in the trade union struggle and also in the advance towards socialism, believers and non-believers work side by side.

"A priest can be friends with communists, socialists, anarchists, agnostics. Fortunately, this is already an indisputable fact in many cases.

"The priest, like any other citizen, should be a participant in the task of building a society without injustice."

Displeasing though this may be to the *ultras*, the attitude of wide sections of the people towards the Communist Party has undergone a profound change, in the sense that we are recognised as a real force against which no one has any right to discriminate, not even those who do not agree with it or who are politically or ideologically opposed to it.

Furthermore, many people who do not say this, nevertheless think it.

In this situation broad circles of opinion are coming out against the persecution of the Communist Party and its members.

The Communist Party, though it is underground, is already a great political party, a mass party whose viewpoint is undoubtedly shared by millions of Spaniards. In Spain today, intelligent people, whatever their opinions, recognise that the Communist Party is the best-organised and most effective political force, and a force of the future.

We have won this position by our history, our correct and open policy, our unswerving tenacity in struggle, and the loyal and heroic behaviour of thousands of Party members.

We have won it, also, by means of the strength we receive from the fraternal ties we maintain with the international working-class and communist movement, which is playing such a decisive part in the transformation of human society and the maintenance of world peace.

The Communist Party is struggling to occupy a legal place in Spanish public life, a right which, for its part, it neither denies nor disputes for any other party. It is ready to accept the rules of the democratic game and evolve within their framework. Today it is acting underground not because it wishes to, not because it enjoys conspiracy and mystery-making but because the dictatorship forces it to. From this situation we shall emerge, together with all the democratic forces, in joint struggle. And we shall emerge, not by anyone's gracious permission but because with our own shoulder-muscles we are throwing off the burden of oppression, drawing ourselves up to our full height and appearing more openly every day, revealing our true shape and our real lineaments in the free air.

THE STRUGGLE FOR SOCIALISM TODAY

Text of a speech made by the author to a meeting of the Executive Committee of the Communist Party of Spain, held in the first fortnight of June 1968 to discuss the Party's attitude towards the Budapest meetings of the Preparatory Commission for the International Conference of the Communist movement.

THE STRUGGLE FOR SOCIALISM TODAY

Sharpening of the General Crisis of Imperialism

The Communist Parties are starting to prepare for the Conference in Moscow. Everything goes to show that the meeting will be a step towards the unity of our movement. The communists of all countries are faced with a whole number of fundamental and profoundly interesting questions in this connection. It goes without saying that there will be no attempt to sit in judgment on, much less to excommunicate, any of the sections of the communist movement, including those which for one reason or another do not yet find it possible to attend. We understand, on the contrary, that decisions must be open towards these Parties, and their collaboration must be sought on all or part of the points of agreement reached, with the aim of bringing about the widest unity of action.

The Conference and the preparations for it offer the opportunity to discuss and go more deeply into a series of ideas and problems that have been brought to the surface by the upheavals caused by today's social and political crises, which are occupying the attention of millions of revolutionaries and, for that matter, of ordinary folk. The whole process should provide for a broad, free and fruitful interchange of ideas.

I stress the *broad* and *free*. It is a fact that vast masses in every country today are endlessly discussing the problems that face them and directly affect them. The term "dialogue" has become the fashion, and actually there has never been a dialogue so extensive as today's. We cannot start from the

101

the idea that we Communists have ready-made answers to all the questions which the masses—and life itself—are posing, and that there is no need to think about anything new. Such an attitude would remind us of the (Spanish) socialist leader who, in the eve of the revolutionary movement of 1934, when asked what the programme of that movement was to be, replied that the PSOE (Spanish Socialist Workers' Party) had formulated its programme in 1908 and that this was sufficient. Life, the experience of today's struggles, are overflowing with new factors. To tackle them, to find solutions for them, we possess a sure guide—Marxism-Leninism. But that, and nothing more than that : a *guide*. Not a rule-book with ready-made answers.

In face of new problems one can adopt a rigid, dogmatic attitude like that of the above-mentioned socialist leader. Or an open-minded, searching attitude, making an effort to come to grips with the new factors and new forces, striving to integrate and unite, avoiding inaction and isolation. This is the frame of mind in which we are approaching the Conference and the preparatory work for it.

In view of what is happening in today's world, we must ask ourselves if we are not facing a new sharpening of the general crisis of imperialism. And whether the reply is "No" or "Yes"—but especially if it is "Yes"—then what are the most disturbing weaknesses in our thinking, in Marxist-Leninist thinking?

Some years ago, when dogmatism and subjectivism, linked with the cult of Stalin, held sway in our movement, we had unchangeable formulas that assured us, with no apparent flaw, of the downfall of capitalism and the victory of communism. All problems were "automatically" solved. When these leading-strings fell to bits, we lost the joyful certitude with which we had approached every problem. We began to ask ourselves questions—which truly was, as the French say, the beginning of wisdom. But at the same time some of us, unnerved by our earlier unthinking approach, moved over to the defensive and left the offensive in the hands of bourgeois thought, bourgeois ideology. It is worth asking ourselves if the fear of subjectivism did not involve us in the risk of an unenterprising "objectivism" that left a lot of territory open to the incursion of the extravagant prophecies and illusions put about by the ideologists of neo-capitalism.

For years they have been deafening us with their hymns about the "affluent society" in which "classes and class struggle are becoming blurred" by the "integration" of the proletariat into the "system" and by the "levelling process". They have been chanting in all keys that neo-capitalism possesses the "mechanisms" necessary for the "control" of economic, social and political development; that revolutionary crises and revolutions are "impossible" and that by means of co-existence we are marching towards an osmosis of capitalism and socialism, towards a "revolution" *sui generis* quite different from what Marx, Engels and Lenin envisaged. The "ageing" and "sclerosis" of Marxism have been noisily proclaimed.

All this commotion had repercussions in our ranks; some people lost their nerve, others became confused. Above all where the Communist Parties were weak and did not have firm roots in the masses, the confusion was serious. In some cases, revolutionary perspectives faded into the distance, if they did not disappear entirely. The immediate practical and political tasks, the *movement,* to some extent became ends in themselves. While this was going on, was the necessary Marxist thought given to discern a series of warning signals indicating the onset of a new crisis of capitalism, deeper and more serious, charged with revolutionary potential? In order, in short, to take the offensive against bourgeois ideology, not by subjective affirmations of faith but by investigation and criticism, so as to raise the militancy and confidence of the Communists and the masses? One must ask whether certain manifestations of "leftism" in some countries are not objectively a product of the dissatisfaction produced by this state of affairs—that is, by the fact that

Marxist thought was questioning itself, paralysed between fear of sinking into the former superficial subjectivism and the apparent risks involved in plunging with creative imagination and passion into the very heart of the events that could be foreseen.

One of the results of the preparation for the International Conference and of the Conference itself must logically be an open recovery of the initiative, an open resumption of the offensive in the ideological struggle. The Conference must be the signal for the economists, philosophers, sociologists and all who are engaged in the ideological tasks of the Communist movement, to engage boldly in investigation and struggle in order to demolish one after another the arbitrary build-ups of bourgeois propaganda and provide a satisfactory Marxist explanation of present problems.

A turning point: the defeat of U.S. imperialism in Vietnam
There are signs of a turning point in the international situation. What is bringing about this turn, and bringing the general crisis of imperialism to its sharpest peak, is without any doubt the heroic and glorious struggle of the Vietnamese people, supported by the Soviet Union, the socialist countries and progressive and democratic opinion throughout the world against U.S. imperialism.

Following the defeat of fascism in the Second World War, extraordinary advances were made, such as the triumph of the revolution in a series of countries in Europe and Asia, the victory of the Chinese and Cuban revolutions, and the process of de-colonisation. But perhaps none of these was so far-reaching in its consequences as the defeat of the most powerful imperialist state in the world by a tiny country whose proud spirit of independence and freedom has the support of all revolutionary and progressive forces in the world. It seems as if at this moment and in this sector of South-east Asia, the endless accumulation of misdeeds, crimes and villainy committed by U.S. imperialism is coming to a head, while on the other hand the will and determination of the revolutionary, peaceful and progressive forces of humanity are crystallising to halt the reckless career of imperialism towards world domination and oppression.

In assuming the leading and dominating role in the world today and turning itself into the world gendarme of counter-revolution, U.S. imperialism has overestimated its strength and its possibilities and has underestimated the revolutionary and progressive forces, the peoples' will for liberty and independence.

While U.S. imperialism is caught by the throat by the heroic people of Vietnam, its capitalist allies—reflecting the sharpening of their own contradictions—are loosening their ties, dissociating themselves from its policy of reckless adventures, and ever more openly questioning the supremacy of their erstwhile "protector". This crisis of political authority is mixed with a decline in the prestige of the dollar and the world monetary crisis. The United States is financially unable to keep pace at one and the same time with the expenses of the war in Vietnam and its other national and international commitments. Lastly, this whole situation has opened a deep crack in the superficially-united society of the United States, laying bare and exacerbating the contradictions that are rending it and all the corruption of the so-called American way of life.

The imperialist aspect of the United States is seen today by the peoples at its most repulsive, with features similar to those of the Hitlerism so hated by mankind. This society, which boasted of being about to enter the "post-industrial era", of constituting a "model" for the rest of the world with its high living standards, is revealed as a soulless society where scandalous wealth exists side by side with extreme poverty, brutal inequality and utter contempt for man; where political assassination of liberal personalities is so frequent that it becomes impossible to deny that it is a question of a policy that is tolerated, if not actually worked out, by those who control the State. A society which shuts up 20 million Negroes in sordid ghettoes, condemning them to a new version of slavery more humiliating than that of the southern plantations in former times; in which democracy is a fiction manipulated by ignorant politicians and all-powerful gangsters; where God is invoked to cover up wealth and power, and genocide is an accepted instrument of international policy. A society rotten with crime, drugs and every kind of vice and perversion.

This image of the strongest and most developed imperialist State is seen in all its loathsomeness through the prism of the aggression against Vietnam, though it had already been glimpsed in the conspiracies and aggression against Cuba, in the intervention against the Dominican Republic, in the Greek colonels' coup, in the aid to Franco and Chiang Kai-shek, in the murder of over half a million Indonesian Communists, in the protection of aggression against the Arab East and in a thousand other cases. The accumulation of horrors, and above all the aggression against Vietnam and Vietnam's heroic example, have caused a real revulsion in world opinion, above all among the youth, a realisation on the widest scale of what capitalism is and what it represents for mankind, even in its most highly-evolved and developed forms. If the sacrifice of Che Guevara has had such a profound effect among the youth, this is because his personal gesture, quixotic though it may have been, expresses the deep sense of aversion and anger amongst the young against the arrogant legionaries of the dollar, and, in some way, the spirit of an epoch in which the little men, the weak, the apparently defenceless, are unhesitatingly defying the great and powerful in order to defend or win their freedom.

In the United States itself, the aggression against Vietnam and its consequences have profoundly shaken public opinion and given rise to a widespread protest against the excesses of imperialist policy. This was started by the youth, particularly the student youth, but it is spreading among a large section of the people. This explains the unexpected results in the Democratic Party of the primary elections for the Presidency, the success of the almost-unknown Senator for

Minnesota, McCarthy, upholder of peace in Vietnam, and the brilliant entry into the lists of Robert Kennedy, also a supporter of peace in Vietnam, murdered by the dark forces of the war party. This response on the part of the people also explains the sudden access of caution among the Republicans, who entered the previous elections under the banner of reaction and war and now, in the case of Nixon, confine themselves to "support" for the Johnson policy while those behind Rockefeller try to appear as if they are picking up the liberal banner of peace.

It is within the framework of this protest against the dominant trend that we must also view the transformation in the situation with regard to the Negro problem : the loss of confidence in non-violent methods, the existence of a latent state of civil war in U.S. society, the demand for *Black Power*.

Robert Kennedy in his election campaign denounced the divisions in U.S. society and the violence embedded in it, facing up to reality. It looks as if there is the beginning of an awakening consciousness, sought for many long years by the Communists of the United States, alone and clear-sighted in an environment steeped in capitalist ideology, where it was really believed that every young North American had the same opportunity to prosper as a Rockefeller, a Ford or a Dupont de Namours.

In truth, only a new awareness on the part of the U.S. people, and especially of the workers, the youth and the forces of culture, can restore the reputation of the United States as a civilised nation in the eyes of the world, a reputation which has been lost through its policy of racism, domination, crime and war.

The rejection of Capitalist Society
The discredit into which present-day U.S. society has fallen has spread to the whole capitalist world, extending to other countries where the "American way of life" has been introduced.

France, in May and June of 1968, witnessed a powerful mass movement which in many ways was one of protest against, and repudiation of, this kind of society. But this powerful wave that stirred our neighbour has spread outwards to other countries of Europe where the same protest is beginning to appear.

In Italy, the political crisis of the Centre Left, the electoral defeat of the Socialist Party and the victories of the Communist Party, the actions of the students and the workers, are aspects of this deep groundswell which, with greater or less force, is stirring all Europe, shaking the structures of capitalism. In Federal Germany the students' and workers' demonstrations reflect the same phenomenon, though more mildly. The same is happening elsewhere in Europe.

The upheaval has shaken several countries in Latin America, especially those where capitalism is more developed.

Side by side with immediate economic, political and cultural demands, these movements are expressing their disgust with modern capitalist society, a soulless civilisation, the morality of profit; they point towards socialism as the objective which is coming ever more clearly into view in the affairs of the capitalist world.

We Marxists should not be surprised that these movements have brought to the surface anarchistic political and ideological elements, remnants of petit-bourgeois ideologies which seemed to have been left completely behind by the modern working-class movement. It is utopian to think that revolutions are made to a "Marxist blue-print", that the proletariat and the people will automatically fall in with a scheme drawn up and decided by the leading party of the working class, a scheme in which all the attitudes and situations are predetermined and follow a detailed programme. The measure of the depth of this movement is precisely the bubbling-up of diverse ideological elements out of the deep revolutionary current that is shifting the whole of society, bringing to the surface whatever is in its depths—good, bad and indifferent. When revolution starts to stir the petit-bourgeoisie and the medium bourgeoisie, they do not breathe out Marxism-Leninism; they breathe out bourgeois and petit-bourgeois revolutionary concepts. When they take part in a movement, these classes express themselves in their own way, finding inspiration in the ideas of the past, when the bourgeoisie was a revolutionary class and when the petit-bourgeoisie tried to graft its own ideology on the new-born working class. When a crisis breaks out, the past, the present and the future are all mixed up together, and only the advance of the revolutionary movement can strain off the old sediment that has been stirred up and replace it with new ideas. When Raymond Aron, trying to combat the movement that has started up in France, speaks of it as "a revolution with archaic tendencies" and writes : "What has come to the surface is a mixture of the old principles of French socialism, Proudhonism and 'Poujadism'. . . ." he unwittingly gives proof of the depth and revolutionary power of this upsurge, which has brought up from the depths of the national history all the revolutionary ideas from one period and another, to match the breadth of the movement.

Marx, Engels and Lenin all spoke of the tendency for revolutions to draw inspiration from earlier models; people and groups engaged in revolution need a model, a point of reference, and each makes use of the one nearest to hand.

But for all its diversity and confusion, the movement in France was an undoubted condemnation of capitalist society, and expressed a general turning, more or less conscious in one or other sector, towards socialism.

How forcefully these movements have shattered the myths that the ideologists of capitalism have been peddling so assiduously all these years ! How vividly they have revealed the strength and vitality of the revolutionary ideas of Marxism-Leninism ! In a matter of days, of hours, they have succeeded in making nonsense out of the monotonous chant about the "ageing" and "sclerosis" of Marxism.

The masses have exposed the falsity of the opportunist and neo-capitalist theories which declare that class divisions and class struggle are "tending to melt away" in neo-capitalist society, that workers' struggles are becoming "de-politicised" and "purely economic"—a kind of "prime mover" for capitalist development—and that state monopoly capitalism "possesses" all the "mechanisms" required to "foresee" and "control" crises and ensure economic and social progress.

These movements have also shown up the falsity of certain other theses, according to which it is impossible for crises and revolutionary situations to arise in highly-developed capitalist countries, that co-existence "suppresses" revolutionary crises and that these are "impossible" without war.

The whole arsenal of revisionism and bourgeois opportunism, which has not been without effect in these years, even in the ranks of some Communist Parties, causing uneasiness, swerves to left or right, and symptoms of anchylosis, has suffered a serious defeat in this whirlwind, the most direct and immediate origin of which is the U.S. defeats in Vietnam.

The Rebellion of the Youth

In this situation the working class affirms itself as the class which must, by reason of its situation in society, its weight and organisation and its revolutionary consistency, lead and direct the struggle for a new, socialist society. Its tremendous power is manifested when it awakes, unites and struggles. All the pseudo-theories that capitalist success has generated in recent years, which deny any such role to the proletariat, are being disproved by events. In this sphere, too, Marxism-Leninism is receiving a fundamental confirmation.

Apart from this, the most significant aspect of the present struggles is the tremendous part played in them by the youth, so significant that it is the object of all kinds of sociological and political analysis—often highly subjective

110

and inconsistent—and we keep hearing about "the rebellion of the youth".

Why is the youth in revolt?

It is not easy to reply without a deeper study of all the factors involved. But right at the start it can be stated that all revolts, all revolutions in history, though they may have been the culmination of class struggles, have had young people in their front ranks. In this respect there is nothing new or exceptional in the present events. The youth are more militant, more generous, less conservative by nature, and they are the first to devote themselves wholeheartedly to the struggle for liberation.

But this does not go far enough as an explanation for the widespread scope of the phenomenon. We must take into account a factor which perhaps plays an essential part in the present "rebellion of the youth".

The concept of human needs, economically speaking, is a historical concept that varies with the development of society and from country to country.

The needs of the slave, then those of the serf, and those of the first industrial workers, were not the same as the needs of the workers today. Historical progress has been modifying them, greatly changing them. In recent decades, this change in the concept of human needs has accelerated at a dizzy speed with the progress of science and technology and the organised struggle of the working class.

Those generations that have watched this acceleration, who have known times when conditions were worse, who contrast their former conditions with those of today, may find it easier to feel content with what has been gained, and may even fear to slip back and lose what they have achieved in the event of a return to the past. (I am not, of course, speaking of the conscious Communist vanguard.) The worker who wore *alpargatas* (rope-soled sandals) and now wears leather shoes, who went about on foot or by bicycle and can now aspire to a car, who scarcely ever went to theatre or cinema and can now have both in his own home

111

with the television, is more likely to feel satisfied and better appreciates the progress attained, the change in his living conditions. Perhaps his notion of the new necessities of life is less sharp. But this is in any case a transitory situation that ends when the progress made in a given period has been assimilated by society, when what has been gained has become quite customary and leads to the birth of new needs, which serves to underline the essential problem—still unresolved : the existence of a dominant class holding on to wealth and power. Even in present conditions, one cannot generalise about the members of the older generation, since a great number of the people who make up this generation— and this is particularly obvious in Spain—have not yet reached the level that the progress of the productive forces should entitle them to, and live in a state of deep and continuous dissatisfaction.

For the younger generation, who were born in the world of the motor-car, the refrigerator and the television set and never knew the old conditions, what has been attained naturally does not have the same significance. This generation feels the need to advance, to go beyond the levels attained to achieve broader and more complete progress.

When the father or the grandfather tells his son the old story : "At your age I didn't have your opportunities", the young folk do not understand; or at any rate they do not regard this as a valid argument.

The younger generation is faced with the fact that, regardless of historical progress, they are up against the same restraints, the same obstacles, essentially speaking, as those of the past, restraints and obstacles that stem from the capitalist system. They perceive that though there has been progress—and precisely because there has been such progress their perception of the contradictions and injustices which persist is all the sharper—there are still glaring inequalities, widely differing standards of living and, above all, a minority social class which owns the basic wealth and retains the entire power of decision in its own hands. Certain improvements have come about in human life, but they have not removed social inequality, they have not done away with the oppression of man by man, or the existence of alienation. The irrational nature of capitalist society, which destroys a great part of the social wealth and stands in the way of better progress, is very clear.

This generation has another advantage over previous ones, which enables it to understand more quickly, to mature faster : in general it is more cultured, having been born in a society in which the demand for development has led to a greater extension of education and in which the information media, with their universal scope, are—notwithstanding the way in which they are controlled and oriented—an instrument of culture, and ought to be even more so.

The youth of today learns from television not merely pop songs or the glories of football but about geography, racial conflicts, class struggles, revolutions, the achievements of science.

The thirst for progress and freedom that grips the new generations is more easily understood when we remember that we are living in an era in which the rapid and impressive advance of science is bringing about a change in human boundaries, a change so extraordinary, for example, as that involved in the overcoming of the law of gravity and the conquest of outer space. The tremendous possibilities opened up by technical progress give to man, and to the youth above all, the sense (which is true) that there are no insuperable limits to what can be done by human intelligence and will.

Nevertheless, these limits do exist. They are the social differences, the class barriers erected by a minority that retains the ownership of the means of production and exchange which exist in society and which ought to belong to society.

At the same time, this new generation has been born and is growing up in a world of transition from capitalism to socialism, of transformation from the industrial revolution to the new scientific and technological revolution, a world

113

which is changing enormously. In other epochs, when human progress from one generation to another was well-nigh imperceptible, it was possible to repeat the motto of resignation, "Life has always been like this and it always will be." Today, this passive, conservative spirit is inconceivable. The man of today knows that life never was like this and that tomorrow, in a year, or five, or ten, it will not be like it is today. And he does not confine himself to saying so; he also knows that the changes and transformations that are taking place depend on what he himself does, what mankind does.

Socialism has a tremendous influence on this new generation. In the past, when socialism was the aspiring figment of clear and revolutionary minds but not a social reality, bourgeois ideology suffused everything. Today the existence of the Soviet Union and the socialist camp, their successes, their consequence, and even their problems and difficulties and the way in which these are exploited by the bourgeois information media, act as propagators (not always voluntary) of socialist ideology. Even though the fact that socialism triumphed first in economically backward countries has given rise to complex problems in the development of the socialist system, socialism nevertheless strikes the youth as being a superior form of society in which man possesses ever more freedom to determine his own and the collective development.

The young come to realise that if the United States or other economically-developed countries were socialist instead of capitalist, mankind would not be enduring the poverty, the difficulties and the threats which today hang over it.

Socialism is the only kind of society which can solve today's problems. Without socialism, how will the great number of backward countries that exist in the world today overcome their lack of development? Without socialism, how can a situation be brought about in which the developed countries will really help, instead of exploiting, the under-developed ones? How are we to bridge the gap between the haves and the have-nots which is today one of the great problems of mankind?

Without putting an end to imperialism, how can we eliminate the threat that thermonuclear weapons entail for mankind, and utilise this energy as the extraordinary productive force it is? How put an end to the anguish—often unconscious but nonetheless real—that permeates the most varied manifestations of modern life, from art to juvenile entertainment?

The restrictions of the religious counsel of resignation, which formerly shackled and alienated the young, urging them to renounce the earthly goods possessed by a privileged minority, have also been resoundingly smashed, and the religious movements are trying to swim with the contemporary revolutionary current in order to outlive class society.

The youth of today in its great mass is objectively tending to become a great revolutionary force. The working class and its vanguard Party should rejoice at this extraordinary flowering of youthful energy, at this historic victory which is forcing the most conservative forces in the world, the most tenacious defenders of the capitalist *status quo*, to try and present themselves as reformers and even as "socialists".

Position of the student and the intellectual in present-day capitalist society

The newest and most original aspect of this "rebellion of the youth" is the attitude of the young generation of students and intellectuals. What is happening in this section of society must be seen as part of the general state of mind among the youth, and particularly as a consequence of the profound changes that modern production is bringing about in the situation of this particular section of young people.

The scientific and technical revolution is changing social structures and modifying the situation of the different strata of society. For example, in the developed countries, it is reducing the specific weight of the peasantry, whose number is decreasing rapidly. In contrast, the class of wage-earning

115

workers is on the increase and is acquiring ever more social importance. Thus also, the scientific and technical revolution is transforming science into a direct productive force. In one way or another, it is bringing the great mass of the intellectuals into contact with modern production, either directly or through the services.

Under the old-style capitalism, the intellectuals and students were a very small social group, associated with the capitalist minority both by their origin and their role in society. The great majority of students and intellectuals were integrated with the bourgeoisie.

The students were the *gilded youth*, remote from and opposed to the working class and the people, an élite fostered by capitalist society for its own continuation and development.

Those intellectuals and students who went over to the revolutionary camp were outstanding individuals, white blackbirds, cursed and vilified by their own class and received with exhilaration and rejoicing by the proletariat, who saw in these isolated cases a confirmation of the justice of their cause and a valuable aid in their struggles.

Marx, Engels and Lenin, the men who gave the working class its decisive weapon of revolutionary theory, were themselves generous-hearted individuals coming from the ruling classes, men whose genius enabled them to anticipate and foresee the future.

But today what was once an individual phenomenon is becoming a collective one, which cannot be understood unless we take note of the structural changes that have occurred.

These are, that the students and intellectuals of today are not the gilded youth of former times. They are not the children of a small privileged social minority. True, the proportion of workers among them is ludicrously small, and is one of the causes of protest against capitalist teaching and universities. But the vast majority of the students, the future scientific and technical cadres and the intellectuals

116

in general, come today from the middle strata, from the petit-bourgeoisie, the medium bourgeoisie, civil servants and intellectuals. So their future is not so secure as it was in other times; what they will inherit from their parents is no guarantee for the future, even though their present living standards may be higher than those of the workers. Even in middle class families today, the provision of education for all the children creates economic problems which affect the student and impel him to claim a whole series of professional and social improvements, confronting him here and now with the need to act as a militant force.

Today's student has to prepare himself to march through life on his own feet and not on papa's. And the nearer he gets to the beginning of his career, the more this need looms up.

Finally the student, when he ceases to be a student, and joins one of the professions, finds himself, like the worker, obliged to present himself in the labour market, to offer his labour power to the capitalists who rule this market, to take his place as another cog in the capitalist "production machine" and become a wage worker. The professional man is as alienated as the worker, subject like any worker to the contingencies of the labour market. Like the worker, on reaching a certain age he can be pushed out of production to become just another unemployed man. Technical advance, in a society more preoccupied to squeeze out all the human energy it can than to re-adapt man to the new techniques and rapid scientific progress, will end by throwing him on the scrap-heap, replacing him with a new labour force, fresh, better-adapted, which in turn after a few years will find itself crushed in the same fatal round of failure to adapt.

The students, and the young professional people and intellectuals, are becoming aware of this social reality and of their actual position in society. In Spain we are witnessing the growth of this awareness not only as shown in the student struggle, admirable in so many ways, but in the ever sharpening tendency towards the creation of organisations of *young* professional people and intellectuals for the simultaneous presentation of their economic, political and social demands—*young* engineers and technicians, *young* doctors, *young* lawyers . . .

And we also find evidence of this awareness in the way these organisations are beginning to link their activities with those of the Workers' Commissions, with whose aims they are identifying themselves more and more resolutely.

They are also conscious of their alienation and are coming up against the restrictions and injustices of a society divided into classes.

What we Spanish communists call the *forces of culture* are objectively becoming one of the motive forces of the revolution, as a result of the changing structure of modern society.

This is a new phenomenon, characteristic of the present day, which we Marxists, when we labour under the influence of previous analyses—correct in their time but now superseded—sometimes find it difficult to grasp.

Whereas in fact, if in the past we joyfully welcomed those intelligent and generous individuals who broke away from the ruling classes, how gladly should we ring triumphant bells today for these remarkable reinforcements that come to the working class at such a decisive moment of social development!

This new, objectively revolutionary social force which is taking shape and becoming more clearly defined, is a reinforcement both in *quality* and *quantity*.

In quantity, because the body of students and professional people has undergone a colossal growth in this century and is still growing. In the developed countries it is a matter not of thousands or tens of thousands but of millions. According to published figures, the student population of the United States has grown in ten years from two and a half million to seven million. In federal Germany it has grown from 110,000 to 500,000; in Britain from 216,000 to 418,000 and in France from 200,000 to 680,000. In Spain, there are about 140,000 students, not counting those who are studying for their *bachillerato*.* This is a tremendously important mass reinforcement.

In quality, because the integration of the students and intellectuals into the revolutionary movement brings with it an element of culture and enrichment of revolutionary thinking, and creates the possibility of an easier revolutionary transition, with less resistance; the possibility, too, of building the new society with the active participation of qualified scientific and technical personnel—without the upheaval created by the need to improvise, or the unavoidable promotion of inexperienced technicians who have to acquire the knowledge they lack in the process of doing their job, using a hit-and-miss approach which is not always successful. The intelligentsia which previous revolutions had to train and create through years of hard work in order to carry out their tasks of construction, can thus take part from the first moment in forthcoming revolutions.

The growing consciousness of the great mass of students and young intellectuals, precisely because it is a collective and not an individual matter, takes place among tension and clashes, amid a ferment of ideas and initiatives which contain contradictory and anarchistic features, advances and retreats. It should be remembered that when the working class began to take shape it too had anarchistic currents and Luddite tendencies, comparable in some ways to what we see today among certain student groups who talk about *smashing everything*. This is a sign of immaturity which in present circumstances can quickly be overcome thanks to the universal influence of Marxism.

Quite often the actions of the students have a strong appearance of being a struggle between the generations. This is because, though their actions are part of the revolutionary process and are essentially the result of social con-

* The Spanish equivalent of the G.C.E.

tradiction and class struggle, the young people of today approach revolution by way of repudiating the ideological and social attitudes of their parents. Each of these youngsters —or at any rate the great majority of them—asserts himself by opposing his progenitors. Only when their actions become linked up with the proletarian movement do these young people become aware that the problem of the conflict between generations only arises in the stratum where they originated, not in the whole social body. Only then do they realise that the struggle of the young against the old is not the struggle of boys against adults or old men, but the struggle of the new, the ascendent class against the old class of the oppressors which is doomed to disappear, that the division is not one of age but of social class, of awareness.

These collective and often noisy characteristics of the growing consciousness among the students can be—and frequently are—used by neo-capitalist ideologies to try and refute Marxism, denying the revolutionary role of the working class and reducing the dialectic of human progress to a struggle between generations, totally disregarding the repudiation of the social system as an objective of the struggle. At times, too, the understandable generosity and impatience of the youth can momentarily leave the way open for provocation.

It cannot be denied—nor should it surprise us—that this new force, as it reaches the threshhold of a revolutionary attitude, brings with it anti-communist prejudices from its family and social background, prejudices which can be exploited by the enemies of the revolution.

But it would be crass error to assume that these prejudices are identical with the rooted anti-communism of the bourgeoisie, even though they sometimes resemble one another externally; the prejudices of the youth are a residual element, an outer shell which can be quickly shed as experience is gained in the course of the struggle.

When Marxists, when communists find it difficult to grasp and understand this new phenomenon, when instead of going out to welcome these new forces, getting together and uniting with them, they get upset by the result of the immaturity of the young people and draw back from them, leaving the field wide open to the capitalist ideologists and provocateurs too—when they do this, they are spoiling their own chances of influencing them and may even behave unjustly towards a section of the youth that merits our respect and attention.

We communists must not treat these new forces either with adulation or paternalism. We must treat them as adults, striving to give adequate replies to the question they ask us, speaking in their midst inasmuch as communist students and intellectuals are part of that movement, and also from outside.

The basic question that has to be hammered out with them is not who has the principal role; the principal role indubitably belongs to the working class, and most of the students and intellectuals recognise this, at least in theory.

There is a whole range of more real and practical questions. Whilst in some European countries—France, Italy, Spain—the working class is organised, possesses great revolutionary traditions and is largely under the influence of the Marxist-Leninist party, there are other countries of Europe where social-democratic influence clearly dominates the working-class movement.

In such countries, the working class has not yet become fully aware of its revolutionary political role. Because of this, it is still not, in actual fact, the revolutionary vanguard. What must be understood is, that so long as the working class does not acquire this consciousness, there will not be a revolution; that no section of society, however advanced and conscious it may be, can replace the working class and take over its leading role; that the foremost task of revolutionaries is to make the working class conscious of its mission.

In these countries the Communist Party influences only a minority. The real question here is : can the movement of students and intellectuals assist the Communist Party to raise the level of consciousness of the working class and help prepare it to assume its historical revolutionary role? The answer must be yes. The movement of students and intellectuals in these countries can play a very effective part and greatly help the Communist Party to overcome social-democratic influence among the working class if it knows how to rely on the working class youth and the young student forces. The Party will win the masses of the working people for revolutionary change by resolutely bringing in the youth, by being the Party of the youth.

In the countries under social-democratic influence, the fusion of real socialism, Marxist-Leninist socialism, with the great mass working-class movement has still to be achieved, and those young intellectuals who come to Marxism-Leninism are called on to play, together with the vanguard Party, an important part in this fusion—a part which it would be wrong to deny them.

It is of prime importance, therefore, for these sections of young people to meet, co-operate with and wherever possible to merge with the Party. The Party can help bring this about by having an understanding and open-minded attitude; rigidity and failure to understand can serve only to crystallise and give permanence to the anarchist and infantile tendencies among these sections, and rob us of the helpful contribution which they could make.

The Party and the youth must be drawn together in a joint repudiation of bourgeois, opportunist and reformist traditions, at the same time getting rid of infantile deviations.

In those countries where the Party and the revolutionary forces of the working class are highly-developed, and there is a revolutionary tradition in the working-class movement, an attitude not of paternalism but of respect for the university youth also requires us to tell them quite frankly that if there are any among them who think they can go on playing the role of an élite in the revolutionary movement, of a political aristocracy in relation to the workers, their Party and their organisations, they are mistaken. The fusion of the movement of students and intellectuals with the Party and the workers' revolutionary movement does not mean in this case the fusion of socialism (as a theory) with the workers' movement—that has already been achieved a long time ago. These young people undoubtedly have a lot to learn from the Party and the working-class movement. Among other things, they can get a clearer idea of the value of organisation and discipline, of the tenacity, consistency and firmness which are characteristic of the proletarian movement, and a clearer conception of social reality and the tactics of the struggle to transform it. Any claim on the part of this new force to be superior to the working class would produce "ultra-proletarian" reactions and result in greater difficulties for the much-needed alliance.

The Communist Party should open its doors to the best and most conscious members of this mass of students and young intellectuals; it should promote dozens and hundreds of leading cadres from among them, not only for specific work among their own circles but for the entire work of the Party.

On the other hand, the question is asked, exactly how should these sections be organised? It would be absurd to imagine a political party specifically made up of students and young intellectuals. But the old-style professional organisations do not seem satisfactory either. Our experience has shown that the Democratic Student Union and the organisations of professional people cannot confine themselves to purely professional matters; they are forced to tackle the problem of the university structure, of the position of their profession in the social system, and through these a whole series of problems related to the entire organisation of society—which leads to politics. We have sometimes referred to these groups and to the Workers' Commissions as socio-political movements. In actual fact the mass organisations, to the extent that they reject the existing social and political system and demand a radical change in it, cannot avoid taking part in politics and must collaborate in this field with the parties whose aim is the victory of socialism.

As the revolutionary situation approaches, the whole of society becomes politically sensitised, and this awareness cannot find expression solely through the actions of the Communist Party and other political groupings. It has to find a wider framework in the mass organisations, which then link immediate demands with the demand for radical political and social change, action for immediate demands with political action alongside the Party and the other groupings, bringing about, through these new forms of action, the political sensitisation of the broadest mass of the people.

In many countries today, the revolt of the students and young intellectuals is still, as it were, molten lava which has not yet solidified, in which varied and contradictory elements are mingled. Whether this force will grow quickly and take the right road depends to a large extent on the work of the Communist Parties.

An attitude of reserve or suspicion towards them can only lead to a lessening of our influence; an intelligent, revolutionary attitude, on the contrary, consists in taking advantage of this great awakening of the youth to broaden the Party's membership, to renew and rejuvenate it, for we are the Party of the revolution and thus—no longer only in words but in life—the Party of the youth.

Alliance of the forces of Labour and Culture
This change in the structure of society caused by the development of the scientific and technical revolution poses the problem of the revolution in Western Europe and the developed countries, with new aspects which began to be tackled at the 20th Congress of the Communist Party of the Soviet Union and which the Communist movement has to develop and enrich by its own experience.

One of the most important new factors occurs precisely in the realm of the driving forces of the revolution and their

124

collaboration for its achievement.

The Leninist concept of the worker-peasant alliance is still correct, and the victory of the revolution in those countries where it has up to now been achieved has been based on it. But particularly in the developed or developing countries, the new social situation of the forces of culture calls for a widening of the alliance of workers and peasants to include intellectuals and students. This means that the achievement of the revolution today brings on to the agenda the need to form what we Spanish Communists have named *the alliance of the forces of Labour and Culture.*

Without belittling by one iota the importance of the peasants and the necessity for a policy of alliance with them, we must take note that at the present time, as far as Europe is concerned, with the technical development of agriculture, the specific weight of the peasantry in society has been reduced. There is no possible comparison between the situation in the European countries, even the less-developed of them, and that which existed in the old Russia and still less with that in China. In the old Russia the proletarian minority got its basic support from the alliance with the vast peasant mass. But in present-day Europe, the salaried workers are already much more numerous than the peasants while the cultural forces have a weight and influence of great importance.

The key to an understanding with the middle strata, an understanding which we have called for in the struggle against the power of monopoly capital, lies to a decisive extent in the alliance of the forces of labour with those of culture.

Intellectuals and students, because of their social origin and position, exercise a tremendous influence on the middle strata, who are generally paralysed by deep-rooted conservative prejudice, who are embedded in the social system and constitute the firmest mass support for the ruling policy and ideology. The experience of Spain in the recent period has shown us that the students and intellectuals, by their struggles, are disturbing the complacent calm, the conformism, the smug satisfaction of the functionary who thinks he is at the summit of society because he is one of the cogs of the system; they are jolting the tranquillity of the petit and middle bourgeois, making him realise that this society is not immutable. They have penetrated into the technical machinery of the capitalist State, the judiciary, even the Army and the forces of public order. They are shattering the conformity of the traditional intellectual circles, the *established* ones.

The students and intellectuals are destroying the influence of bourgeois policy and ideology from inside the social strata which were its support. By so doing they are completing the action of the working class, in the front line of the class struggle, with a flanking movement tending to isolate the supporters of capitalist society, fundamentally to reduce its influence and power, and to help smash this society from both inside and out.

The Communist movement needs to study and rapidly absorb this new reality which is bringing it nearer to its liberating goals and overturning all efforts to make people believe that capitalist society, in its modern forms, has reached a situation where it can control its contradictions and advance in harmony towards further progress.

The alliance of the forces of Labour and Culture is today the concept which corresponds to the spirit of Leninism. It is the sure way to revolution. One might say that in the developed and developing countries this concept also affects the possibility of achieving the worker-peasant alliance, that the peasants will not draw decisively together with the proletariat while the leading class of the revolution has not fully absorbed and understood the role of the forces of culture.

In his speech on the 150th anniversary of the birth of Karl Marx, Comrade Suslov dealt with the new possibilities of alliance and of working class victory in these words :

"The proportion of hired manpower among the gainfully

employed population of the United States and other developed capitalist countries has gone up to something like 80 to 90 per cent in the mid-1960s. The new social groups that have emerged as a result of the scientific and technical revolution and are now being exploited by capital, provide fresh opportunities to extend the front of the working-class struggle for the basic transformation of the existing system. This means that the exploiting class is objectively confronted by the overwhelming majority of the population.

"The Marxist thesis that the bourgeoisie will never surrender their power of their own free will still holds true today. But the experience of the working-class movement shows that the forms of revolutionary coercion can differ depending on concrete historical conditions. The major problem of the offensive strategy of the present-day working-class movement is to bring about objective and subjective conditions that enable the revolutionary masses to do away with the rule of the monopoly bourgeoisie.

"How can these conditions mature? In what way will it be possible to bring the masses to the decisive stage in the struggle against the monopoly bourgeoisie? Such are the crucial questions facing the working-class movement in advanced capitalist countries." (*Brilliant Teacher and Leader of the Working Class*. Report by M. A. Suslov at a meeting in Moscow on May 5, 1968, to commemorate the 150th Anniversary of the Birth of Karl Marx. p. 24. Novosti Press Agency Publishing House, Moscow, 1968.)

New paths in the advance to power

In fact Comrade Suslov's way of posing the problem corresponds to the present tasks of the Communist Parties in the capitalist countries. Ways have to be found to draw the masses into the decisive struggle against the monopoly bourgeoisie. This means that the question must also be posed of the conquest of political power by the democratic anti-monopoly forces. The question does not present itself in the same way in each of these countries; but in various ways and through various phases the Communist Parties must firmly declare their determination to work towards this end. The need is all the greater because, for some Parties, the prospect of the advance to power became more distant and almost vanished during the years of intensive capitalist development that followed World War II in Europe and elsewhere, years in which governmental coalitions of the so-called Centre Left seemed to bar the way to alliances capable of bringing about radical changes on the one hand, while on the other neo-capitalist and opportunist propagandists were more or less consciously putting round the idea that conditions did not exist in the developed countries for the taking of power as had been done in the countries where the revolutions had been achieved.

The stagnation in some cases, in others the slow growth of the Communist Parties during these years, the result of the political and ideological harassment which capitalist advance made possible to the bourgeoisie, also arose from the fact that while previous patterns for the advance to power had had to be discarded, the new possibilities and perspectives were not sufficiently clear. The Communist Party cannot progress and develop its strength unless it has a clear revolutionary perspective. This is an old truth, which from repetition has come to seem a cliché but which nevertheless retains all its vigour and actuality. The *movement* of itself can never be a means of strengthening the revolutionary Party of the working class.

How is power to be achieved in the developed countries? The discussion on this, in a somewhat formal and schematic way, has turned around the question of the peaceful way or the violent way. In the concrete conditions of Spain, certainly, this discussion was neither schematic nor formal, having in mind the psychological aftermath of the civil war of 1936-1939. Furthermore, by stressing the peaceful road as opposed to that of civil war, the policy of the Party in fact resulted, through the development of mass struggle and the perspective of a *national strike*, in raising, developing anew the fighting and revolutionary capacity of the masses, in creating moral, political and organisational conditions for a new revolutionary offensive, after years of oppression and enforced quiescence brought about by the fascist victory.

Nevertheless, what is new and basic in the present situation in the developed countries is the fact that *the working class, provided it builds the alliance with the peasants and the forces of culture, can gather sufficient force to bring about a disintegration of the capitalist State unknown so far in previous revolutions, in a society which is economically ripe for socialist transformation.*

And this power to disintegrate the State can supersede the traditional formula of the political general strike and insurrection.

The experience of the mighty mass movement of May-June in France provides a basis from which to forsee how a radical transformation can be achieved in the developed countries; it shows that a new formula of struggle has emerged which is much more than the traditional political general strike of the working class, without being insurrection as we have witnessed in the past. This formula is the *national strike.*

We Spanish Communists, starting from the actual conditions of the struggle in our country, had worked out this perspective as the way towards overthrowing Francoism and advancing to a democratic, anti-feudal and anti-monopoly régime which would open the gates to socialism.

What we meant by the *national strike* was this : a political general strike by the workers, plus the paralysing of activity in the countryside, plus the closure of the universities and institutes, plus action by the colleges and professional organisations, plus the closure of the businesses and industries of the petty and middle bourgeoisie, plus a strike of civil servants. That is to say, united struggle by all the anti-Franco and anti-monopolist sections of the population to bring about a total paralysis of the country, conquest of the streets, and fraternisation with the armed forces, causing the

129

collapse of the Franco State and opening the way for its replacement by a new system of government supported by the people. We had foreseen that the people in the streets would have to use force in some cases to overpower centres of resistance set up by the régime. This means that while we envisaged forms less violent than civil war, we did not rule out the possibility of a degree of armed confrontation. This is why we have welcomed—and more than welcomed, initiated and encouraged—the most energetic response to the forces of repression in mass actions through which we consider that the conditions for the national strike are being created. In our perspective, we deliberately differentiate between the *political general strike* and the *national strike,* regarding the first as the means of unleashing and furthering the second.

The experience gained in our country—of the forms of struggle of the working-class and the student movement, of the movement of the intellectuals; the participation of priests and Catholic movements; the formation of Commissions of small and medium businessmen and industrialists—all this showed the correctness of what we envisaged and clarified it still further.

But the powerful workers' and popular movement that shook France in 1968 has shown even more clearly the prospect of the *national strike* as the way, combined with other forms of action and struggle—for example, electoral and parliamentary—to achieve the radical transformation of society in the developed countries.

How did the events in France come about? Starting off with its own demands (in some cases not altogether understandable to the rest of the population), the student movement opened a breach through which the working class, with its formidable weight and organisation, poured in, followed by other dissatisfied social strata.

The students occupied faculty buildings and schools, taking professors and academic staff along with them, and set up forms of mass control which, irrespective of the immediate result of the movement, will remain as an example and an effective method for future use.

The workers came out on strike and occupied factories and other enterprises, putting forward demands which by their magnitude revealed the intention—though still confused in many instances—to make themselves masters of the means of production. The trade union committees, playing a role like that of the Workers' Commissions in Spain, took the responsibility for ensuring the leadership of the movement and the maintenance and protection of machinery and equipment; in this way the working class let it be clearly understood that those instruments of production, which today are in the hands of the capitalists, belong to the working class which intends to keep them in good condition for the time when it will take charge of them once and for all.

There are certain aspects of the working-class struggle which have special significance. Thus, for example, the printing workers, in many cases along with the journalists, saw to the publication of the newspapers, censuring them—as was the case with *Le Figaro* when the news it carried misrepresented the true situation and the aims of the movement—and even preventing the appearance of some publications—such as the Gaullist *La Nation*—when they opposed this.

The gas and electricity workers ensured regular supplies for the population as a whole in order to keep ordinary life going on, thus showing their ability to run these services and their high degree of class consciousness.

The railway workers who occupied stations and depots completely paralysed all traffic; but in some instances they took the initiative of organising special trains with specific social aims, showing their ability not merely to organise a stoppage but also to ensure the functioning of the service.

Other sections, for example postal and communications workers, also occupied offices and completely stopped services. At one stage the strike was joined by the technicians

131

responsible for communication between the Ministry of the Interior and police headquarters, an extremely delicate and important part of the State apparatus.

In a modern State, radio and television constitute one of the most decisive instruments of power. Journalists, programme planners, producers, artists, technicians and other working personnel took control of the broadcasts, taking them out of the hands of the authorities for a time and placing them at the service of society in the name of objectivity and freedom of information.

There were capitalist newspapers where the journalists demanded changes in the structure of ownership which would give them the power of decision over the orientation of the paper—a profoundly democratic demand.

Although it is very difficult to find out exactly what happened in the armed forces, it seems certain that a good part of the police forces objected to being used for the violent suppression of the movement; and one police union published a declaration right in the middle of the strike which expressed the discontent among that force.

It also seems to be true that even in the General Staff there was for a time opposition to intervening against the movement so long as it did not go outside the democratic framework within which it was developing.

Significant, too, is the judgment of the Paris magistrates who during the events rejected the claims of the owners of Citroen against the occupation of their factories by the workers.

All this means that the mighty popular and working-class movement in France illustrated, on the one hand, the deep interpenetration of democratic and socialist slogans; while on the other hand it showed that what we call the alliance of the forces of Labour and Culture possesses a power unknown to the revolutionary movements of other periods, a power to dissolve and disintegrate from within the organs and springs of power of the modern capitalist State.

This State, at its present level, has become so highly

132

technical that it depends far less on the repressive will of a group of politicians, military and police chiefs committed to repression, than on the personnel which in practice handles the machinery of State and can decide whether it functions or is paralysed.

This, probably, is why General de Gaulle said that at one stage the situation had become *insaisissable*, impossible to grasp, and impossible for the authorities to control.

In France the objective and subjective conditions did not yet fully exist for the development of the national strike to its final conclusion, that is, the establishment of a political, anti-monopoly power which would open the way to socialism. But the French example has shown, more than any other so far—and it is not the first time in history that the French workers have set an example to those of other countries—the possibility of bringing about the disintegration of the capitalist State, of seizing power largely from the inside as well as from the outside, which is made possible today by the changes that have taken place in the social structure, and the awakening of broad masses of society, united with the working class, to the evils of the capitalist system. What was interesting and also new was the way in which the attack on the capitalist superstructure became intermingled, fused, with democratic and socialist demands, the fact that demands which on the face of it were purely democratic became imbued with anti-monopoly and, in the last analysis, socialist content.

The French example has shown that this path of the *national strike* can make insurrection in its well-known classical forms, unnecessary.

Nevertheless, this new, much broader, more democratic way of taking power by the revolutionary forces of society does not exclude the use, at a given moment, of a certain amount of violence.

In every revolution there necessarily comes a moment at which the old system of government is broken, at which the new takes over and definitely establishes itself. Up to that moment, the revolutionary forces are taking over (sometimes from within) various sectors of the apparatus of State power: the factories, the services, press, radio and television; but if this movement does not culminate in the seizure of the central power of the State, in a word with political power, nothing will have been consolidated and when the tide turns the positions taken must be abandoned and bourgeois political power takes them over as it regroups its forces.

If the French Parliament, instead of a reactionary Gaullist majority, had had a working-class and left-wing majority, then the masses in the streets would have been able to impose on Parliament the formation of a government that reflected the popular movement; this government, relying on the positions of power seized by the masses and on parliamentary legality, would have been able to begin the transformation of the State apparatus, thus crowning the achievements of the masses of the people. Even then, the possibility could not be ruled out that centres of armed resistance might be formed by the bourgeoisie and the most reactionary groups and these might have to be overcome by revolutionary force. The points of similarity between a national strike and the classical insurrection, together with the important differences between them, are determined by the bourgeoisie's ability and determination to use force in defence of their privileges.

Thus it becomes ever clearer that what we have called *the peaceful way*, more with the idea of stressing its democratic nature and its difference from the classical insurrection and civil war than because of its real content, cannot—in the conditions existing in Spain, needless to say—be a way that is simply electoral and parliamentary.

This is why the formula of Comrade Suslov is correct when he says that *"the forms of revolutionary coercion can differ depending on concrete historical conditions"*. An exclusively electoral and parliamentary way cannot lead a country to revolution, at least so long as the socialist system is not the unquestionably dominant one in a world scale,

134

and for this to happen it will be necessary for the revolution to have triumphed already in a number of developed countries.

This does not mean that in those countries where political liberties exist the electoral and parliamentary ways should be underestimated, and still less that they should be pushed to one side. That would mean sinking into the most primitive anarchism. The electoral and parliamentary ways in these countries are a component part of the struggle to obtain power. Revolutionary action can be transferred at a given moment to the electoral field, and may reach a decision or finally consolidate itself in that field.

In the course of the national strike, the revolutionary forces may be drawn into forms of violence among which barricades should also not be excluded. In recent strikes and demonstrations that have taken place in Spain, workers and students have sometimes set up barricades to protect themselves against the forces of repression. This old form of struggle should not be regarded as having been definitely relegated to the cupboard of history; life itself shows that it can still be useful.

This is not to say that power today can be won from the barricades. The battle of the barricades, in itself, is a purely defensive tactic which leaves the enemy the initiative for taking the offensive. But in certain cases the barricades can help to undermine the morale of the forces of bourgeois "order" and can help to neutralise them and even win them over—even if only in part—to the side of the democratic and revolutionary forces. Engels wrote in 1895 that it was mainly this point of view that would have to be taken into account in the future when considering the possibility of eventual street fighting. The formula of the *national strike*, as a means of bringing about a radical transformation of society in the developed and developing countries, is one of the acquisitions of the Communist movement which must be assimilated and developed in the present period.

Work in the Armed Forces

In capitalist society the army and the forces of "public order" are the final "argument" of the system against the forces of democratic and socialist transformation. As the bourgeoisie feels itself becoming weaker it glorifies and exalts the role of the Armed Forces as defenders of the "social order". The reactionary parties, as they become impotent, abdicate from their functions in favour of the Armed Forces, who are removed from their real job—national defence—and given a political role, and who use the weapons the country has placed in their hands to protect it from external aggression, in order to suppress and subjugate it.

The struggle against this monstrosity does not end with criticism of the deplorable role that capitalism has assigned to the Armed Forces, nor with the denunciation of the eventual excesses committed by them. The influence of the reactionary parties who try and compel the Army and the police to play this role must be challenged inside these forces. Democratic and revolutionary influence inside these forces, though it may extend to only a minority of the commanding officers may, in a revolutionary situation, result in the neutralisation of these forces and might also cause a section of them to go over to the side of the people.

The Communist Parties, the revolutionary forces, must not under-estimate the importance of this task, otherwise they may well find the road closed to them. This does not mean that the task has to be seen in the same light as in other periods, when work among the armed forces was called "anti-militarist activity". Today, this work must start from recognition of the necessity of the army and its role in dealing with a foreign threat, which is real so long as imperialism exists, and the need for the forces of public order in order to cope with anti-social elements who are not exactly the forces making for the transformation of society but rather reactionary elements, ready to provoke civil war in order to perpetuate their privileges, besides those who cannot be induced to adapt themselves and who exist in all societies and will continue to do so for a long time to come.

The "other ranks" continue to be the main objective of this work; for at the opportune moment they can change the attitude of the Armed Forces and prove decisive in bringing them over to the people's side. Systematic propaganda and organisational work among them, adapted in each country to the situation there, is obligatory. Reaction will always try to denounce such activity as subversive; but the democratic and revolutionary forces must carry it out for the sake of guaranteeing the right and freedom of the people to take up such political and social options as best suit its interests and national development.

But at the present time there exist much wider opportunities than in the past to extend this work to officers and commanders.

Officers and commanders in the developed countries—and in Spain as well—are no longer recruited basically from among the sons of the aristocracy nor even from the military caste. A military career is no longer an occupation for unemployed aristocrats or wealthy playboys.

With the development of the new techniques, it is a career that is becoming more *intellectual*, more *scientific*, requiring much wider knowledge. Furthermore, the educated military man today finds himself required to study the problems of so-called "subversive war"—that is today, a people's war of liberation, the prospect being that wars which may break out in these days may be met with a liberating reply, which can occur also in States that set out to make war with imperialist aims. In such study, the military man will encounter Marxism, the problems of social and national liberation, although this encounter initially takes place from a hostile position.

It must be stated that the movement for renewal which is being witnessed in Catholicism, if it does not arise from this is nevertheless being strengthened by the need of Catholic theologians and scholars to study what there is in Marxist theory which can mobilise and transform society, a theory

137

they can no longer ignore even for the purpose of opposing it. They are having to study Marxism because of its successes and its revolutionary advances which are threatening the influence of the Church. The encounter with Marxism has accelerated the crisis in the Catholic Church and the movement for renewal within its ranks, as well as drawing many Catholic priests and laymen closer to the revolutionary movement.

If this is happening in an organisation so traditional, hierarchical and isolated from progressive influence as the Church, it is by no means impossible for it to have some effect on the Army and the forces of public order, particularly their best-educated and most thoughtful elements. The selfsame Catholic evolution can also affect some military cadres.

What in some countries is called Nasserism is to some extent a reflection, though it may be primitive, embryonic and confused, of the clash between the old military mentality and the new social problems.

This state of mind can develop favourably. The military cadres, who mainly come from the middle strata, are not exempt from the problems of those strata nor are they inoculated against the profound trends towards renewal which are permeating society today.

The decision must be taken to carry out systematic work among them. To be effective, this work must not be mere "political agitation". It must deal with their real professional problems, their demands, as well as with questions concerning military doctrine, national in character, which have been abandoned by the ruling classes; it must deal too with the change demanded by modern technique and the lines of national military policy. That is, the work among these sections should be given a positive, constructive orientation. More than in any other institution or stratum of society, we must show them not only what present society fails to offer ——more directly in relation to their own role and function—— but also what we ourselves propose to do and how to do it,

138

and how we envisage the future relationship between the people and the Armed Forces.

Certainly in each country, depending on the actual situation, the nature of the work in the Armed Forces can vary. But what the Communist Parties and the revolutionary forces in general *must not do* is to fail to challenge the influence of reaction inside institutions which, in a revolutionary situation, can play a decisive role according to which attitude they adopt.

The requirements of the pluralist way

In the present historical situation, the Communist Parties in the developed or developing countries need to work out an offensive policy that provides a democratic and socialist alternative to the state system of monopoly capital. An essential condition in working out such a policy is clearly to link the intermediate stages of the struggle, the immediate objectives, with the perspective of the conquest of power by the revolutionary forces.

Even when the Party is not yet more than a small minority, its work in pointing the way towards this prospect is fundamental for its development. Every member needs to know the relationship between the battles he is waging today and the broader and more decisive battle for socialism. When this perspective is not clear, the *movement*, the intermediate stages, become the essential thing, and the Party runs the risk of appearing to the masses as part of existing society (and not the most effective part) rather than its negation and the instrument of its overthrow. The danger of stagnation and immobility becomes a real one.

Today the Communist Parties in the developed countries are upholding the concept of political pluralism in the advance to socialism, as distinct from what happened in other revolutions that took place in other circumstances. But this pluralist concept must be further developed, in order to cut the umbilical cord connecting it with the Stalinist thesis of a single party. In practice, the idea of a proletarian party

139

which is not only the *leading* but the *dominant* party is still very much alive—and can be exacerbated by the attacks of other parties on our own—and results in attempts to claim the leading role for the Party in present struggles in a unilateral, exclusive manner that stems in fact from the notion of the *single, dominant* Party.

But the concept of pluralism implies that the role and capacity for initiative of other groups must be recognised, not only on the attainment of power and as a voluntary and gracious act of dispensation, but also in the course of the struggle which leads the revolutionary forces to the conquest of power; it implies that effort must be made to integrate this capacity for initiative and this special role into the revolutionary advance as a whole; that from now on we have to find room for diversity and the contradictions that stem from it.

The leading role of the Party, therefore, becomes more complex, because it has to combine and harmonise its initiative with that of others; it has to learn to reckon with other initiatives of various hues, in the common leadership; it must learn to use the activities of other forces, not in a narrow partisan sense but in the sense of ensuring their positive participation in the development and progress of the revolution.

The leading role of the Party will in this way be established, not by partisan claims to superiority, not by exclusiveness in the working out of correct decisions, nor by imposing them, but by the ability to harmonise the actions of the different revolutionary forces whose agreement is needed; by the ability to bring about unity, to give way on minor issues in order to safeguard the main one—the unity of the revolutionary forces for the taking of power. In these conditions the Party grows stronger not by unilateral affirmations of its own superiority but by its capacity to unite and to demonstrate in action, to all concerned, the need for revolutionary political choices. The Party's maturity and ability to lead is judged on the basis of its ability to provide a policy of unity. It is along these lines that the road can be opened to the real possibility of a pluralist socialist society.

To be victorious in such a situation does not mean showing up the incapacity of other groups; it means helping to bring them to a common understanding of reality.

More than ever in these conditions, the mass organisations must not be regarded as *transmission belts*, but must become active participants in the steering of the revolutionary process. Instead of being an instrument through which the Communists mobilise and direct the broad masses, they must be transformed into a platform that will enable the direct representatives of the broad masses to co-operate with the Communists in the guidance and leadership of the revolutionary process. It follows that these organisations must have an active political function, alongside the Communist Party and other revolutionary political groups, complementary to their own specific actions as mass organisations in their particular field.

This road towards revolution is much more democratic than the classical one, for it includes much broader forces; therefore it is less violent both before and after the taking of power.

The Battle of Ideas in the Pluralist Socialist Society
The pluralist way also presupposes the possibility that different forces will be able to agree on the need for a socialist society—a society in which the basic means of production and exchange are social property—without having reached identical views on all aspects of ideology. Otherwise a multi-party system would not have any meaning. From the moment when full agreement existed in the ideological field and Marxism-Leninism was accepted without reservations, a multi-party system would become pointless.

A process of development like this is understandable, because the progression of the economic structures of State monopoly capital brings out the social character of production and clearly reveals the incongruity of this social character and the existence of private property. This aspect of reality is more easily appreciated than other aspects of our ideology, and can mobilise sections of the population who have not yet identified themselves fully with Marxism-Leninism in support of the economic and political forms of socialism.

But this way means that the social and political forces of socialism will be brought into being without Marxist-Leninist ideology being made "official", with wide cultural freedom and with the ideological struggle going on inside socialist society. And it will continue not only as a struggle against the political and social enemies of the new system, but also as one between its supporters and those who co-operate in building the classless society; a struggle between friends, between comrades sharing the same basic cause.

We must recognise that this implies coexistence between different schools of thought, a coexistence which does not exclude struggle. We are convinced of the final victory of Marxism-Leninism. But this victory will be achieved through a big, long-drawn-out, peaceful discussion of ideas, without intolerance. As a result, too, of the experience gained in the new society, as an effect of the transfer to the level of human consciousness of the triumph of Communist economic and social structures.

This is a vital aspect of the new opportunities that are now opening up in the world—and particularly so in Spain—for drawing religious trends and movement into the struggle for the conquest and construction of a socialist society.

In this confrontation, this lively battle of ideas, the vitality and influence of Marxism will be strengthened not by official or administrative measures but by the enrichment resulting from the progress of science and culture and the effect of the new structures on the human mind.

142

Unreserved acceptance of this method is a pre-condition for the multi-party road to socialism; it is also a pre-condition for the credibility of the multi-party choice by other forces. Without it, we should deserve the opinion, and the exploitation of this opinion by the class enemy, that this path was just an opportunist manoeuvre; and we should be erecting fresh obstacles or adding to existing ones, standing in the way of the advance to socialism.

The great teachers of Marxism have repeatedly stressed the necessity for not looking backwards, for not mechanically copying the revolutions of the past; they have insisted that each revolution has its own specific features, its own original aspects. But mechanically copying previous revolutions does not mean disavowing them : it means being conscious of the fact that their very realisation has brought today's possibilities of revolution to a new and higher level. To be faithful to them does not mean to try and imitate them in every detail, it means to continue the advance, starting not from their positions but from the new position which their existence and their victory provided for us.

In this connection the fight against dogmatic catchwords and against the way the content of these catchwords lingers on in the new approaches that present day reality demands, is one of the most characteristic ways of upholding the living essentials of Marxism-Leninism. The international Communist movement, in tackling its present tasks, has to face these problems and get right to the bottom of them.

Problems of the "Third World"

The world revolutionary movement today is made up of the countries of the Socialist camp which, with the Soviet Union in the forefront, constitute its advance guard; of the working-class and progressive movements in the developed capitalist countries; and of the anti-imperialist liberation movement in the countries of the so-called Third World. Revolutionary ideas today possess an enormous strength which is seen everywhere, many-sidedly, penetrating and covering all social strata, all aspects of life and culture. Believers are in the habit of saying that "God is everywhere", and it can be said today that revolutionary ideas are to be found everywhere and that it is impossible to stamp them out. When imperialist reaction thinks it has defeated them in one place, they break out in another with greater force and violence. At times these ideas are unwittingly let loose by the *sorcerers' apprentices* who attempt to juggle with the people's destinies.

To unite, co-ordinate and harmonise the different components of the world revolutionary movement is one of the most important and delicate tasks of the present time; that is why it is particularly important to strengthen the alliance between the Socialist States, the revolutionary working-class movement in the developed countries and the anti-imperialist liberation movement.

A great problem of the present period is the gap between the material development of the economically advanced countries and that of the under-developed ones. All the economic studies show that, if capitalist and imperialist structures continue, this gap, instead of diminishing and disappearing, will go on getting wider and deeper in a most menacing fashion. According to one U.S. study, the average per capita income in more than 40 under-developed countries of the world is less than 120 dollars a year, while in the United States it is 3,000 dollars. A Hudson Institute study forecasts that in the year 2000, while the United States, Japan, Sweden and Canada will have an average per capita income of between 4,000 and 20,000 dollars, today's under-developed countries will not exceed the figure of 200 to 600 dollars. As long as the imperialist system continues, the gap between some countries and others will become ever deeper and wider.

Capitalist ideologists and some of their pseudo-left hangers-on use this situation to try and do away with the division of the world into exploiting and exploited classes, into imperialist countries and countries which are socialist

144

or are following a non-capitalist path of development, and create instead an arbitrary division between industrialised, rich, surfeited countries—regardless of their social system—and poor, needy, hungry ones. In this way they try to disrupt the alliance between the socialist countries and the under-developed ones, between the working-class in the capitalist countries and the peoples of the Third World; they try to cloud and obscure the responsibility of imperialism for this situation of inequality in the development of different peoples.

Thus they conceal, for example, the fact that U.S. imperialism takes out of the Latin American countries far more dollars in imperialist profits than it sends in in the form of "aid". At the same time they conceal the fact that in Europe itself U.S. capitalism also takes out many more dollars than it puts in, and is practising a sort of colonisation of this continent, actually making use of European capital for this purpose.

So long as imperialism has not been wiped out, the problem of real and effective aid from the developed countries to the under-developed ones, so that within a given time they may attain that levelling-up which the productive forces make possible today and which justice demands, will not be resolved. The international conferences which are continually held on the problem can work out partial measures (which they do as a result of the combined pressure of the socialist countries and the under-developed ones) but these will always be partial measures that do not go to the root of the problem.

The capitalist countries, and above all the United States, are today expending the money which could be used for real and disinterested aid to the under-developed countries on increasing their enormous war budgets. Faced with this colossal arms drive on the part of imperialism, the socialist States—and especially the Soviet Union, which has a basic role in the defence of the socialist camp—are obliged to devote enormous resources to defence as well. And as socialism has been victorious so far in countries whose development was backward, and not in the wealthiest and most developed ones, those countries have to invest great resources in the construction of a modern economy which can compete with and as far as possible surpass capitalist economy, and all this obviously affects the degree of material aid which can be given to the under-developed countries.

The wiping-out of the inequality between countries cannot be seen except as connected with the victory of the revolution in the developed countries. That victory would represent an immense aid to the revolution in the under-developed countries and to the modernisation of their economy.

Nevertheless, even today, the help of the Soviet Union and the socialist countries to the under-developed countries is of great importance in the struggle against neo-colonialism. This help differs radically from the "aid" which the imperialist States say they give, because it is directed towards promoting the development of an independent national economy, with its own industry, while imperialist "aid" is designed to get rid of its "surplus" output and is, moreover, accompanied by economic strings that mean increased exploitation.

The success of the economic development plans of the Cuban socialist revolution is an experience of great value for the countries of the "Third World". The entire world revolutionary movement is interested in this success, which will show once and for all how under-development can be rapidly overcome by following a socialist path, and with the help of friendly States.

At the present time, there is a need to give far more attention to the working out of a theory in the economic relations between the socialist countries and the under-developed ones which are following a non-capitalist path of development, and to pay more theoretical attention to ways of overcoming the inequality between developed and under-developed countries. These problems are of vital interest not only to those who live in the under-developed countries but to all those in the developed countries who are concerned about the future of humanity. Multitudes of sociologists are writing about these problems—some well- and some ill-intentioned—and are coming up with the strangest theories. The repercussions that these theories can have, even momentarily, among wide sections, simply indicates the depth and urgency of the problem. The forthcoming Conference of the international Communist movement needs to sharpen the interest of Marxist theoreticians in tackling and studying these problems more deeply, for they are problems of great importance in the world today, and can be exploited by enemies of Marxism if they are not dealt with by Marxists in a thorough and satisfactory manner.

The Revolution in the Under-developed Countries

It is clear that the problems of the revolution and the tactics of revolutionary struggle have quite different aspects in the under-developed countries.

In many of these countries, an extremely weak bourgeoisie depends almost wholly on the imperialist power which directly or indirectly dominates it. The proletariat, as a class, is little developed. The intellectuals are a small section of the population and the great mass consists of the peasantry.

In these countries the question of national liberation is closely tied up with that of the liberation of the oppressed classes. It is impossible to separate one from the other. Thus, nationalism becomes not merely an ally but a component part of the struggle for revolutionary emancipation. It is quite wrong to label nationalism in general as a counter-revolutionary factor when in numerous countries where struggle against imperialist oppression is essential it acts as a revolutionary one. Revolutionary tasks are determined by the objective situation; we have to start

147

from things as they are and not as we revolutionaries would like them to be.

Each revolution gets its strength and its weaknesses from the specific national context in which it is forged. This context cannot be altered at will. In an article about a Guatemalan revolutionary who fell in the struggle, Ché Guevara tells a relevant story from the Cuban revolution :

"*El Patojo* (the Duck)—the nickname of this guerrillero— had been in at the birth of the project for the revolution in Mexico; what is more, he had offered himself as a volunteer; but Fidel did not wish to take any more foreigners on this national liberation undertaking in which I had the honour to participate."

He goes on to say :

"I repeat, Fidel did not take him, not because of any negative qualities, but to avoid making our army a mosaic of nationalities."

In fact the Cuban revolution, which became a socialist revolution, inspired by profound international sentiments, triumphed within the framework of a national situation and as a profoundly national revolution. This is a characteristic of all revolutions, particularly those in countries oppressed by imperialism.

Very recently we have seen the attitude of the leaders of the glorious liberation struggle of the Vietnamese people towards the offer of volunteers from the socialist countries, the Communist Parties and other revolutionary movements. Without refusing the offer in principle (lest it should become necessary to accept it at some later date) the Vietnamese leaders have kept their struggle strictly within the limits of a national struggle, led and directed by themselves. Considering their undeniable experience and political wisdom, it can be concluded that the Vietnamese comrades have powerful reasons for acting in this way. Without doubt the principal one lies in their anxiety not to "internationalise" the battle but to preserve all those factors that emphasise its national character and enable them to mobilise all sections of their fellow-countrymen.

In some under-developed countries the numerical weakness of the proletariat, which usually carries with it a weakness of political consciousness and cultural backwardness, is such that the leading role in the national revolution seems in some cases to be taken by progressive elements among the intellectuals—or to be shared between them and the most enlightened proletarian elements. In a number of cases the leading role of the working class in these revolutions is exercised indirectly, by reason of the importance of this class in the world revolution as a whole, the influence of Marxist-Leninist thinking among the progressive élite and the international weight of the socialist States. This explains why, in some under-developed countries, the birth or consolidation of a leading Marxist party takes complicated and original turns, and why it may happen that the revolution is initiated even before the formation of such a party.

The special characteristics of these countries, in particular the preponderance of the peasantry, the embryonic condition of the State apparatus, the inadequacy of communications and geography itself, cause the guerrilla struggle in certain conditions to become a highly important form of revolutionary struggle, provided the people are prepared to wage and sustain it and provided it is combined with other forms of struggle and with the task of disintegrating the forces of repression at a time of crisis, in which a general desire for political and social change materialises.

The experience of the patriotic revolutionary struggle of the Vietnamese people is, in this sense, the most conclusive of its kind. It holds valid lessons for all oppressed peoples :

1. The art of putting in the forefront the national demands which are capable of uniting the immense majority of the people, and consequently, the ability to direct the blow against the main enemy.

2. The ability to combine military guerrilla action with the political action of the broad masses, who do not

149

take part in the armed struggle but contribute to it by their political and other demands; liaison between political and guerrilla strategy.

3. The ability to create the broadest possible national front, disdaining no ally, undermining the bloc of enemy forces, neutralising some and winning over others.

4. The art of utilising all imaginable possibilities and methods to mobilise world opinion in their favour and even, at a given moment, to carry on the struggle while negotiating with the imperialist enemy, so as to isolate him and confront him with world public opinion (and public opinion in his own country) and force him to withdraw.

In the majority of the under-developed countries, there is no other prospect of liberation—at least so long as the forces of world imperialism have not been decisively smashed—save armed struggle. Most of these countries have no authentic democratic tradition, and all but a few have been governed only by representatives of the feudal landowners, subject to imperialism and using the most brutal methods of dictatorship and tyranny.

The Struggle for World Peace and European Security

Other questions are still as important as ever in present circumstances. Such, for example, is the struggle for peace, and as regards our continent, for European security. The basic object of this struggle is to prevent a world confrontation between the Great Powers, a confrontation which today would take the form of nuclear annihilation. The policy of co-existence which we uphold is based on this need.

Practice has shown that the defence of peace and a policy of co-existence does not and cannot signify the maintenance of the social *status quo* in the world. The example of Vietnam is an illustration of this. The Soviet Union and the socialist countries are giving vital help to the Democratic Republic of Vietnam and the National Liberation Front

150

of South Vietnam in their war of liberation against U.S. imperialism, and this help is not in any way hindered by the policy of peace and co-existence. On the contrary, it can be said that the victory of the Vietnamese people over the U.S. imperialist aggressor is becoming one of the most far-reaching and decisive contributions to the peace of the the world.

Just now, negotiations are taking place in Paris between the representatives of the fraternal Democratic Republic of Vietnam and those of the United States Government. We communists whole-heartedly support the position of the Government of the Democratic Republic of Vietnam. In the initial phase it is endeavouring to impose on U.S. imperialism a cessation of bombing and other acts of war against North Vietnam. Later, the real negotiations can begin, to achieve the withdrawal of American troops from South Vietnam, ensure the right of self-determination for the Vietnamese people and re-establish peace in Southeast Asia, in accordance with the programme of the government of North Vietnam and of the National Front in the South.

These are difficult negotiations, which may have to continue for a long time and encounter setbacks. It is evident that the U.S. has failed to defeat the people of Vietnam despite having concentrated an army of over half-a-million men there, equipped with the most up-to-date and frightful weapons and assisted by about 100,000 mercenaries from satellite countries and the 700,000 mobilised by the puppet rulers in Saigon. It has also been shown that a people resolved to lay down life itself for liberty, in present-day conditions, with the existence of the Soviet Union and the socialist countries, cannot be defeated by imperialism. And it has become evident that between the desire of the United States to act as the gendarme of counter-revolution and its actual capacity to fulfil this hateful role, notwithstanding its industrial and military potential, there is a great abyss. On the other hand, the experience of the liberation war of the Vietnamese people

151

has confirmed that it is possible to defeat imperialism and force it back to its lair without unleashing a thermo-nuclear world war that would bring death to all mankind.

The Vietnamese people's fight for freedom has not by any means come to an end with the start of conversations in Paris. The fighting in the South is increasing; the barbarous bombing-raids by U.S. aeroplanes continue to destroy towns and take human lives in North and South; napalm continues to sear the bodies of women and children, anti-personnel bombs sow death among the civilian population. The very city of Saigon, seat of the puppet government of Thieu and Ky and of the high command of the invading forces, is being destroyed, district by district, by the U.S. bombers. A strange way to "liberate" a country!—by destroying its occupied towns and slaughtering their inhabitants. This is what Hitler's troops did in Warsaw!

The U.S. aggressors have earned the scorn of the whole world, arousing the same condemnation, the same sacred anger of the peoples as that aroused by the Hitlerites guilty of genocide 25 years ago, which brought them to defeat and catastrophe.

U.S. imperialism has already lost the war in Vietnam on the ground. The Tet offensive is the military and political Dien Bien Phu of the U.S. invaders.

Despite this, the U.S. rulers are intriguing and manoeuvring to obtain round the negotiating table what they will never win on the field of battle. We can have full confidence in the tried and tested firmness and wisdom of the leaders of the Democratic Republic of North Vietnam and the National Liberation Front of the South. They will know how to combine military action in the field of battle with diplomacy round the negotiating table. But our duty is to help them, mobilising the Spanish youth and the Spanish people ever more widely in their support, overcoming the narrow and excessively conspiratorial methods employed by the Spanish solidarity movement and throwing it wide open to all our fellow-countrymen who desire peace and freedom for Vietnam, whatever their political and religious views.

Freedom and peace for the people of Vietnam represents a new stage in the people's march towards the destruction of imperialism, towards liberty and socialism.

The solidarity of the masses the whole world over with the Vietnamese people's struggle has contributed to the isolation of U.S. imperialism, to the puncturing of its arrogant domination—as seen in the crisis existing in NATO and in the military pacts set up by the Pentagon generals.

An even more important contribution has been the solidarity of the socialist countries and particularly the Soviet Union. The Vietnamese combatants are fighting with modern Soviet rifles, machine-guns, tanks, artillery and rockets, which give them an offensive and defensive capacity against which the massive array of American war material has shattered itself.

The manoeuvring of the American negotiators, who are prevaricating interminably in Paris and holding up the progress of the negotiations, demands an ever more forceful reply by the peoples.

The Soviet Union and the socialist countries are also upholding the just cause of the Arab peoples against the Zionist aggression which receives its motive force from the aggressive policy of U.S. imperialism.

The policy of peace and co-existence, then, does not exclude the most resolute help for those people who are fighting for freedom with arms in their hands. This policy is in no way an obstacle to the revolutionary struggle of the peoples.

This struggle surges up and develops wherever people have become aware of their situation and are resolved to make every sacrifice for their freedom. No outside intervention can take the place of the revolutionary decision and energy of a people. It is a hundred times true that revolution cannot be exported. Revolution is born and develops in a

153

national framework, though its basic objectives link it with the world revolutionary movement. Every attempt to export revolution is bound to clash with national sentiment, and this at a given moment could enable the reactionary forces, hoisting the national flag, to mobilise the broad masses of the people against revolution and to present it as something foreign.

This is why we have always stood out against the attitude of certain naive revolutionaries who would have liked to see the United States, *gendarme of world counter-revolution*, opposed by a Soviet Union *gendarme of world revolution*. Thus we stood out against the attitude of those who, in the first days of the Arab retreat in Sinai, criticised the Soviet Union for not intervening directly with troops; we stand out against those who childishly consider that the Soviet Union ought to send troops wherever a guerrilla force springs up or whenever a political reverse is sustained by the democratic forces.

If the Soviet Union had done this, if it had directly intervened with its troops in every country where there has been or is struggle, we should find ourselves today with *national liberation movements*—headed by reaction—in those countries. The export of revolution would have turned against the first socialist State the very movement that is now developing against the United States and decisively threatening its aspirations to achieve world domination.

A policy of direct intervention in every quarter of the globe, utterly foreign to the socialist character of the Soviet regime, would have caused it to degenerate and become transformed into a new Bonapartism.

The Soviet Union and its Communist Party have had the wisdom to maintain a judicious policy of help for those peoples which are struggling, without affecting the national character of that struggle or meddling in the internal affairs of other countries.

It is only imperialism which, because of its nature, can try to assume the role of *world gendarme*. And we are already beginning to see the grievous consequences of this policy for those who pursue it.

In Europe the struggle for European security is coming to the fore with growing urgency. Faced with the growth of the democratic and revolutionary forces, monopoly capitalism is promoting and fostering reactionary and fascist regimes and groupings. Behind all the efforts to unleash reaction stands U.S. imperialism. In Spain and Portugal, it continues to give direct support to the fascist dictatorships of Franco and Oliveira Salazar; in Greece it backed the fascist Colonels' *coup d'etat*. In Federal Germany, Nazism is raising its head and becoming an increasingly serious menace. In France, notwithstanding some disagreement with "Gaullist" policies, U.S. imperialism and its agents support the efforts to reinforce *personal power* against the democratic and working class forces.

Everywhere the manoeuvres of imperialism and reaction, becoming more and more discredited in the eyes of the people, are moving in the direction of giving a leading political role to the most reactionary military groups. These efforts on the part of reaction contain a warlike threat which represents a great danger for peace in Europe and the world.

The most serious political threat, however, lies in the revanchism of Federal Germany which, 23 years after the defeat of Hitler, has become, with imperialist help, the strongest political and military power in capitalist Western Europe.

At Karlovy Vary the Communist Parties of Europe adopted a series of decisions on the struggle for European security which still hold good and which require further effort to put into practice, seeking the collaboration of all the forces of peace, democracy and progress.

"Left" childishness

If present events are giving a crushing answer to the neo-capitalist sermons and the opportunist deviations of the right, and showing that capitalism is a social system doomed

155

by history; if these events are confirming that the working class is the class which can, in alliance with other classes and groups of working people, sweep the capitalist system away, it is no less true that what is happening also proves the correctness of Lenin's criticism of the infantile deviations of the "Left".

The danger of these deviations is that, objectively, they contribute to the isolation of the proletarian vanguard from the majority of the sections of society and from their natural allies without whose co-operation the victory of the revolution is impossible. Engels was right when he stated in 1895 that :

"The time of surprise attacks, of revolutions carried through by small conscious minorities at the head of the unconscious masses, is past. Where it is a question of a complete transformation of the social organisation, the masses must also be in it, must themselves already have grasped what is at stake, what they are going in for, body and soul." (Marx-Engels Selected Works, Vol. 1, p. 134, English edition.)

In fighting against infantile extremism, we Communists must recognise that it arises not from the subjective will of this or that irresponsible group but from real and deep objective causes.

When a society is ripe for political and social change, on the eve of these changes there arises among certain sections of opinion a sense of impatience, a kind of yearning to push things faster. This state of mind, positive in essence, leads to the emergence of groups expressing these impatient feelings, and at the same time provides opportunity for those in power to commit acts of provocation designed to discredit revolutionary ideas and delay their victory.

Such a situation is a test of the proletarian Party's ability to lead, and it must be able to distinguish between the honestly impatient people and the provocateurs, but above all to maintain contact and some degree of control over the impatient ones, so as to cherish and utilise all that is positive and militant in them (which can be a great deal) and integrate them in the common struggle.

Only the development of the struggle, open and honest political discussion, the courage to combat the enemy without flagging but argue with the misguided friend—not taking offence at his unjust criticism but meeting it with the lessons of concrete experience—can help us to overcome "leftist" difficulties.

In any case, we Communists should never forget that *the real enemy is to the right of us*; this will help us to unmask the direct agents of that enemy who try to outflank us from the "left".

On the other hand, if we consider the social breadth which, for example, characterises the struggle against the Franco dictatorship in our country, it is inevitable that certain non-proletarian sectors, certain groups of limited scope, should intervene in this struggle with methods and forms which do not have the mass characteristics of the proletariat and which we should not copy. Although it is our aim to achieve common tactics and objectives for the whole of the opposition, we cannot deny the possibility that certain forms of struggle which might, if they were employed generally and used by us, be counter-productive, may serve to awaken and mobilise social sectors over whom we have little influence and thus objectively serve the anti-Franco cause. The important thing is to show in practice that the methods and forms of struggle that we regard as the most effective really are superior, and that it is with them that genuine political and social change can be won.

The manifestations of infantile "leftism" have different aspects in different countries. In Spain, for example, one of the manifestations of "leftism" consists in the counterposing of the *struggle for socialism* to the *struggle for political liberties*, and an underestimation of the importance of economic and industrial demands.

Those who take up the "leftist" position mistakenly hold that in Spain political freedom is one of the battle-cries of

157

that section of the bourgeoisie called the neo-capitalists, and is therefore an instrument of neo-capitalism. They seem to forget that the Falangist press is also trying to make out that the demand for political liberty is a manoeuvre of the Opus Dei* bourgeoisie to grab power from the Falangist "revolutionaries" who have held it for thirty years, talking about "revolution" but serving the bankers, the big industrialists and the landowners.

Genuine revolutionary feeling in Spain today is shown not by verbal condemnations of capitalism nor by the exaltation of a vague and misty "workers' power" which is counterposed to our slogan of winning for the people freedom and the power to decide their own destiny. *The touchstone of revolutionary feeling today is effective struggle against the Franco dictatorship to abolish and destroy it.*

In face of this fundamental task, any underestimation of the value of political freedom, in the conditions of the Franco dictatorship, constitutes an aberration which can only be considered *señoritil*—worthy of some pampered young offshoot of the aristocracy. The winning of political freedom in a fascist country is a pre-condition for attaining the possibility of developing the full strength of the masses of the people who want more profound changes. The struggle for political freedom is the only genuine and serious way to develop the class struggle and go forward to socialism.

Spanish capitalism has historically demonstrated that political freedom stifles it. This is why it installed the brutal dictatorship which our country has endured for years, and why it provoked the civil war of 1936-1939. Neither traditional capitalism nor those groups which (more out of mimicry than anything else) call themselves "neo-capitalists" really want political freedom. At the very most they aspire to a sort of vague liberalism, and even when they talk about

* The powerful Roman Catholic lay organisation, members of which control most of the banks and industries of Spain and many of the seats in General Franco's cabinet.

158

democracy, echoing the people's longing for freedom, they are incapable of drawing the logical conclusions that would have to be adopted in the realm of political action.

The fact is that monopoly capitalism as a system—not only in Spain—has shown its antipathy for democracy. Even in those western countries which have traditionally enjoyed political freedoms the tendency today is towards restricting them, if not openly abolishing them. Monopoly capitalism threatens all the political liberties regained in the war against fascism in the whole of Western Europe. In France, the Gaullist *coup d'etat* of 1958 made further substantial inroads into the democratic liberties that had already been eroded by the governments of the Fourth Republic. Since the great popular movement of May and June this year (1968), Gaullism is threatening to go even further in restricting these liberties, and is spurring on the re-constitution of various reactionary and fascist organisations, copying Franco's "slogans" against Communism.

In Federal Germany the adoption of special powers seriously threatens the few existing political liberties, while Nazism again raises its head, fostered and encouraged by the powers that be.

Against the reactionary policy of monopoly capital, the longing of broad sections of the people for liberty is a powerful force which objectively meshes with the objectives of the Communists and revolutionary forces and which it would be stupid to underestimate.

Political liberty and democracy are of far greater concern to the workers than to the bourgeoisie.

"Left" infantile attitudes on this question basically coincide with the Menshevik position that Lenin and the Bolsheviks had to contend with. The Mensheviks held that the democratic revolution was the concern of the bourgeoisie, and was the task of the bourgeoisie. Lenin maintained that at that period the democratic revolution was of fundamental concern to the proletariat, which must struggle for the leading part in that democratic revolution.

159

At the time of the struggle against the monarchy in our country, the reformist leader Julián Besteiro was against the participation of the working class in the revolutionary movement which—though momentarily unsuccessful—carried the Republic to victory, on the grounds that the Republic was mainly a matter for the bourgeoisie. This attitude, ostensibly a "class" one, was typically reformist.

The conquest of political freedom in Spain today is of concern first and foremost to the working class, to the forces which aim to transform society. Those who genuinely want a socialist Spain have to understand that to get it they must fight directly against the dictatorship and for freedom.

Another typical sign of "left" childishness is the under-rating of economic and professional demands. This under-estimation reflects, on the one hand the influence of neo-capitalist theories on these "leftists", and on the other an academic, bookish notion, reformist at bottom, about the nature of *revolutionary education.*

The way neo-capitalist theories have impressed these "leftists" is shown when they talk about the economic struggle as an "integral part" of the capitalist system, which acts as the "motive force" of monopolist development itself, leading to the concentration of capital and the expansion of production.

But economic and professional demands do not in actual fact objectively play such a part. When Spanish workers demand a minimum daily wage of 30 pesetas or more, a month's paid holiday, full employment, the 40-hour week and trade union freedom, they are acting not as a "motive force" for "capitalist development" but as a battering ram against the Franco dictatorship and thus against the system of monopoly capital. For it is quite clear that these demands go far beyond what monopoly capital wants to grant or can grant while it sticks to the capitalist principles of "profitability" and "competitiveness". Already in the last century, Marx and Engels stressed that behind the demand of the Parisian workers who from the barricades of 1848 called for "the right to work" lay the implicit demand for the ending of wage labour and capital and their reciprocal relationship. With how much more reason can it be said today, then, that many workers' demands which seem purely economic or professional, express the steadfast desire for the ending of capitalism, of the exploitation of man by man—a desire which would be expressed far more openly if the dictatorship were not there.

In France, for example, the economic demands and those connected with the trade union freedom put forward by the Paris workers in May 1968, went far beyond the limits of the capitalist system and were neither integrated within it nor did they contribute to its development. When economic demands go beyond a certain point—and this is also the case in Spain—they are aimed against the entire social system.

Moreover, the workers would not follow a Party that did not support their demands, that did not understand how necessary it is for a worker to improve his living conditions within capitalist society, when the situation has not yet matured for putting an end to it. If Communists did not resolutely support these demands, they would abandon the field to all sorts of reformist preaching and influence and would cease to guide and organise the working class and consequently the revolution.

But historical experience has also shown that the working class begins and completes its revolutionary growth, comes to an understanding of its historic liberating role, in the course of economic struggle and through the combination of this with political struggle. It is fashionable nowadays to use the term *"concienciar"* (raising the consciousness of the workers). Some leftists declare that all Communists and revolutionaries should devote their entire time to *consciousness-raising*; and they envisage this as working outside the struggle, by means of *pamphlets*. Some of these leftists even question whether it is *ethical* of the Communists to rouse the masses to struggle without first raising their consciousness

161

—that is, without first making them understand (by articles and pamphlets) what socialism is.

This attitude denotes a complete lack of understanding of the situation of the working class in capitalist society : the idea that the working man can come to socialism by the same road as the student and the intellectual, by study and scientific reasoning. Capitalist society does not give the worker a chance to acquire the intellectual ability to come to socialism solely by the path of scientific reasoning. Capitalist society puts the worker in a condition of exploitation, in an inferior social position. The worker struggles against this society from necessity, from class instinct. When he demands higher wages and better conditions, the worker comes into conflict with the capitalist state apparatus, with political power—and becomes fully conscious of the need to overthrow this power and this apparatus and carry out a revolution. Apart from this basic schooling which he gets from the struggle itself, the worker begins to take an interest in science, to try and gain a rational understanding of the scheme of things which he opposes instinctively and as a result of experience. The formation of the revolutionary consciousness of the working class is a whole dialectical process, the mainspring of which is participation in the struggle.

The reformists are always reproaching Communists for wanting to carry out the revolution before the working class is *educated* for it. We Communists reply that the working class educates itself through struggle and becomes revolutionary through struggle and the carrying through of revolution. And an indispensable step towards this is the economic struggle which under revolutionary leadership becomes transformed into revolutionary political struggle.

There are times when it almost seems, on the face of it, as if we revolutionaries were the "reformists" and the reformists were the "revolutionaries". This happens when we fail to give a clear explanation of the intimate relationship that exists between the struggle for political freedom and anti-feudal, anti-monopolist democracy, and the real struggle for socialism; when it looks as though we are putting the struggle for liberty first while they put socialism first, as though we are struggling *above all* for economic demands while they struggle *above all* for revolution.

Against "leftist" childishness in our country there is one basic argument : the struggle. Those who genuinely struggle against the dictatorship, who take part in demonstrations and strikes, who actively resist the excesses of the repressive forces as Communists do, *are ours.* The impatience they sometimes show should not put us off. We have to show them in practice that those who are in the front line of the struggle, who face up to risks and dangers and at the same time possess a correct line and effective tactics, are the Communists. Seeing us struggle they will understand us better. In joint action, in friendly discussion, their ideas will become clearer and closer to our own. Only those who do not struggle, who take refuge in verbal "leftism" so as to avoid struggle, who oppose action against the dictatorship, so as to weaken the mass movement and preach a withdrawal to the catacombs; who try to reduce all work to that of "raising consciousness" by means of pamphlets—the *de facto* advocates of passivity, the charlatans—these, no matter how "revolutionary" and "socialist" their words may be, *are not ours because they are not sincere revolutionaries.*

Keep Close to the Masses

The preparation for the International Conference, and the Conference itself, should help to develop the understanding that we are entering a period of sharpening class struggle, a period which may be harder but which opens inspiring opportunities for the Communist Parties to transform themselves into genuine leaders of the forces of the working-class, the people in general and the youth.

In this period, in very short spaces of time, the Communist Parties can grow and develop to an extraordinary degree, and become great mass parties all over Europe.

163

With this in view, it is highly important to know which and what are the mass forces most ready to adopt a progressive and revolutionary stand; it is essential for us to link up with these forces, and get right in among them. In saying this we are not referring to the hackneyed generalisation that "these forces are the working-class, the peasants and the middle strata". We are referring to the actual movements and groups which are coming to the fore inside and outside the existing parties and organisations and which, though they may not be clear at first about their objectives, are capable of coming towards revolutionary positions of struggle coinciding with ours. The Communist Parties must make a great effort to link up with the youth, with the movement of revolt which is stirring the younger generation; they must rejuvenate themselves and avoid the error of seeming to be just another "traditional" party geared into the political game of the bourgeois establishment.

It is now becoming increasingly important that each Communist Party should know how to use the autonomy and independence which the present structure of the international Communist movement provides, to work out an effective line of struggle against monopoly capital and its rule, for an anti-monopolist democracy, for socialism.

There is no mechanical determinism, no law, which guarantees the Communist Parties a vanguard role in the transformation of society in their countries if they themselves are not capable—strategically and in action—of applying the theory of Marxism-Leninism correctly and creatively.

A revolutionary situation can appear in the developed countries today with specific aspects, with new features which must be grasped, understood and mastered. Neither phrases, nor catchwords, nor sticking to previous revolutions will provide us with solutions to the problem of how to act as the leading force in the present situation. Each victorious revolution has had new features which each Party has had to tackle and solve in an *original way*.

In the struggle against monopoly capital, we must avoid falling into the crude traps laid for us by opportunist propaganda. M. Servan-Schreiber, for example, a theorist specialising in the defence of the European monopolies, tries to ridicule the struggle against monopoly capital by confusing it with struggle against what he calls "strong points"—that is, against the great industrial concentrations able to make use of modern technology. But for us Marxist-Leninists, the struggle against the monopolies, and more specifically against monopoly capitalism, is not a struggle against the concentration and the technological development; on the contrary we want this concentration to be carried out more rapidly and rationally, by eliminating private profit which so often (and particularly in Europe) acts as an obstacle to the process of modernisation, and by socialising the ownership of the basic means of production. A socialist Europe, which Servan-Schreiber sneeringly rejects, would provide exactly the framework in which the scientific and technical revolution could overtake and quickly surpass the level attained by U.S. imperialism.

It should nevertheless be pointed out that our call to the anti-monopolist middle strata for an alliance against the ruling oligarchy in no way conflicts with our call for the democratic and socialist concentration of the means of production and the fulfilment of the scientific and technical revolution; for in present-day Spain—and generally speaking all over Europe—the obstacle to this is not the small and medium enterprises, which play a complementary role in production and can continue to do so, but precisely the monopolist enterprises and their State, which are incapable of fully developing the new techniques.

The Situation in the Socialist Countries

On the eve of the Conference of the international Communist movement, have we—the Parties in the capitalist countries—anything to say about the problems of the socialist countries? Should we express our opinions about these problems or would it be better to keep silent? It does not seem that we can keep silent about problems which also concern us very directly, which are being widely discussed in the capitalist countries through the medium of the bourgeois Press and propaganda. It is equally impossible to remain silent when the comrades of the socialist countries engage in discussion among themselves and directly or indirectly criticise various developments within their countries, and when this discussion leaks out and becomes known in our countries.

We cannot put our heads in the sand and proclaim that in the countries where socialism has triumphed there are no more problems, contradictions or diversity of opinion. Nor must we develop an inferiority complex about it. That there should be problems and contradictions, that different—debatable—options can arise, is a law of development which also affects the socialist countries.

There is one essential point of departure when one starts talking about the socialist countries, and that is the recognition that these countries are the vanguard and the strongest bastion of the world revolutionary movement.

Among the socialist countries, the U.S.S.R. occupies a fundamental place which is determined by history, by the U.S.S.R.'s immense potential and by its international policy.

We Communists regard solidarity with and the defence of the Soviet Union and those countries where the socialist revolution has triumphed as a fundamental duty.

This solidarity and defence is a foremost duty even though we may not share the viewpoints and concepts, methods and particular choices of this or that country. For example, although we disagree with the policy of Mao Tse-tung and the Chinese leaders and condemn their policy of dividing the Communist movement, we should feel in no way less bound to defend the Chinese revolution against any imperialist threat.

What could we Communists from the capitalist countries

ask for in a discussion with the socialist countries?

It seems to us that in the first place—taking for granted the socialist countries' real and effective solidarity with the world revolutionary movement—our most fervent wish is that the socialist countries should advance steadily along the path of assimilating the new techniques of production created by the scientific and technical revolution so as to overtake and surpass capitalism in the sphere of production in the shortest possible time.

To achieve this the socialist countries, despite their high annual industrial and agricultural growth rate, must contend with a handicap : with the fact that the socialist revolution, for well-known reasons, triumphed first of all not in the most developed capitalist countries but in economically backward ones.

The socialist countries, and particularly the U.S.S.R., have achieved spectacular successes in the scientific and technical field. But we consider that no socialist country, large or small, can aspire to develop production of the whole gamut of industrial goods in line with modern technological advances, all at the same time. This is true also of the capitalist countries, including the developed ones, and the discrepancy between the progress of one and another is evident, as is the need for each to specialise in those products for which it is best endowed economically, a factor which objectively imposes an international division of labour.

Is there not a need to speed up the rational division of labour among the socialist countries, a closer voluntary dovetailing in the economic sphere? Is the necessary ironing-out of inequalities in development conceivable without this closer economic integration?

Certainly, the question of economic integration among socialist countries does present difficulties. It cannot be done without careful consideration for the legitimate national interests and sovereignty of each State. There may be resistance, subjective attitudes full of national narrow-mindedness on the part of big as well as small powers. But

167

we consider that in face of the United States and capitalist Europe, where the monopolies are ruthlessly introducing an international division of labour which facilitates technological development, the socialist countries will be obliged to speed up the division of labour and the integration of their economies if they want to overtake and surpass capitalism.

In the second place, we Communists of the capitalist countries are concerned for democratisation and the overcoming of bureaucratic methods of work in the socialist countries. Like all Communist Parties, those of the socialist countries are not immune from errors, and their ability to correct their mistakes is a source for the strengthening of communist influence in the world.

This was proved by the results of the 20th Congress of the Communist Party of the Soviet Union. The denunciation of the cult of the personality, which was the highest example of self-critical courage on the part of a Communist Party, even though it caused some temporary confusion, in the long run led to a powerful reinforcement of communist influence throughout the world. It was the starting point for fresh impetus and fresh growth in the strength of communism.

The recent events in Czechoslovakia, the replacement of the bureaucratic leadership of Novotny and the steps taken to democratise the life of the Party and the State and give the masses a more active part in the leadership of the country, have been welcomed by us Communists in the capitalist countries as an aid to our own struggle.

It is true that the imperialist enemy is still powerful and we must remain on guard against him; that he uses his ideological weapons to try and undermine the socialist countries; that he tries to profit from their contradictions and natural difficulties.

But when all is said and done, it is imperialism that suffers when mistakes are vigorously rectified, and this rectification provides a firmer base for developing the ideological struggle inside both socialist and capitalist countries.

The experience of Czechoslovakia confirms once again that socialism is the system in which democracy—that is, the broad participation of the working class, the intellectuals and the whole people in leadership, comes up against no insuperable obstacles, either ideological or social, in its development. Socialism moves towards more fully democratic forms which ensure for the people the highest level of participation in leadership, forms which need not necessarily, and indeed will not, resemble formal bourgeois democracy, but will be far superior, and based on a fundamental fact : that the ownership of the means of production and exchange is in the hands of the producers. This is the fountain-head of genuine democracy, and it is why socialism means the full attainment of equality of rights and opportunity for all men. These new forms of democracy, though their content will be the same, will have new aspects in each country according to each one's special national features, which will not fade away for a long time to come.

The presence of imperialism, which lurks behind every crisis in our camp to try and exploit it and get something out of it, should make communists cautious and vigilant; but it must not be a barrier to prevent us from admitting and correcting our mistakes so as to increase and consolidate our strength and prestige and ensure the final defeat of imperialism.

On the contrary, it is under the capitalist system and imperialism that insuperable barriers exist to the full realisation of freedom, barriers that leave no alternative but revolutionary change. In the capitalist countries, freedom conflicts and becomes incompatible with the existence of monopolies, of the ownership of all social wealth by an insignificant minority and the control of the State, in one form or another, by this minority.

We Communists, who are a very young movement—compared with the twenty centuries of Christianity we have only just been born—have still a lot to learn in the practice and experience of revolutions. We have to get rid of the old

Utopian notion, shown up as false by Lenin but still ingrained in many of us, that socialist revolutions are all made by following the same pattern. National characteristics, historical traditions, the level of economic, political, social and cultural development and even the errors and successes of the revolutionary forces, create differences which cannot be eliminated by decrees or excommunications or by any communist "Inquisition". Only experience, development, fraternal collaboration and discussion, with mutual respect and the greatest possible understanding of the particular circumstances in which each people and each Party is evolving, will enable us to build a firm unity in the struggle against imperialism, for peace, socialism and communism.

For the creative development of Marxism

The preparations for the International Conference, and the Conference itself, should contribute to a more extensive circulation of ideas and more friendly and comradely discussion within the communist movement. This will lay the basis for an enrichment of our ideological work, for the expansion and triumphant advance of the ideas of Marxism-Leninism.

Undoubtedly the Conference will not be able to solve all the current problems—those enumerated in this report and those which may be causing concern in other Parties. Probably the conditions for this are not yet ripe. Nevertheless, it will constitute a notable step forward if such problems are brought into the open and discussed, examined in the light of different opinions, and if concern about them is extended and deepened.

We are conscious that our viewpoint, as expressed here, may contain mistakes and inadequacies. We do not think we possess the whole truth about all questions by any means. What we do regard as necessary, indeed indispensable, is an actual search for an open discussion of ideas, among comrades.

At the same time it is urgently necessary for our philosophers, economists, sociologists and all workers on the theoretical front to apply themselves more freely and actively to the work of theoretical investigation and elaboration. The overriding aim of this work should be the analysis of the contradictions of contemporary capitalist society and the clarification of the lines of march for the revolution; the exposure and intelligent refutation of the ideological ammunition of capitalism and the strengthening of the entire ideological arsenal of the communist movement.

This job of investigation should not be confined within the limits of the short-term political requirements of the parties, though it may in the long run assist their tactical aims.

In the course of this work there will be mistakes, half-hits and successes; but no investigation is possible that does not accept the risk of error and seek to overcome it. On the other hand, until the results are adequately proved and demonstrated, there is no reason why theoretical researches should involve the Party's official positions.

In conclusion, we stress the need to stimulate a greater flow of ideas, broader discussion, a more audacious and offensive spirit on the part of the Communist theoretical forces, which involves dialogue, polemics, the comparing of positions and the ending of paralysing taboos.

MORE PROBLEMS OF SOCIALISM TODAY

Article published in the theoretical journal *Nuestra Bandera* No. 59, 3rd Quarter 1968.

MORE PROBLEMS OF SOCIALISM TODAY

The military intervention in Czechoslovakia has opened up a new difference in the world communist and workers' movement. It is a question of a difference between communists; a matter which concerns the forces of socialism and progress. The Franco press and information media, which have utilised the event to unleash a campaign designed to discredit the Soviet Union and the cause of socialism, are—in their own interests—on the other side of the barricades, the side opposite to the one we occupy, regardless of our differences, the side of all the Communist Parties whether they have approved or disapproved of the intervention, those of the Warsaw Pact countries, that of Czechoslovakia or our own. There can be no confusion about this. The Franco press is trying for its own purposes, to stir things up; to sweep away the class frontiers and substitute a new frontier, that of a "freedom" which, coming from the pens of those who uphold the dictatorship, smacks of irony. They are wasting their time. However much they put themselves forward as "sympathisers" of a "new" brand of socialism, they cannot conceal their aversion and hatred for socialism, which is what leads them to take advantage of an error in order to fight us with greater subtlety.

Those Communist Parties, including our own, which have disapproved of the intervention, stress at the same time that nothing has altered in our attitude towards the Great October Socialist Revolution, towards the Party of Lenin or

175

towards the Soviet Union. That country's historic worth, the leading part it plays in the struggle against imperialism, for socialism and for peace, are not in question. Moreover, we will combat all those who impugn it. We continue firmly to defend the Soviet Union and all socialist revolutions, which constitute the highest gains of the world working class and the forces of progress.

Those who cherish illusions about the emergence of a "new communism" of a geographical nature, of a "western communism"—like those who once cherished illusions about a "national communism"—are in for a rude awakening.

International solidarity among Communist and workers' parties and the progressive forces should not be lessened by this or that difference; it should on the contrary reaffirm itself until such time as experience, reflection and time help to overcome the differences. We are confronted by an enemy, imperialism, which is showing what it is capable of in its barbarous aggression against the Vietnamese people, in the mass slaughter of Communists in Indonesia, in its support for the regime of the Greek fascist colonels, in the oppression of the Dominican Republic and the threats and provocations against socialist Cuba. Nothing must weaken or lessen solidarity in the struggle against this enemy.

What is happening is that the battle of ideas about problems relating to the strategy and tactics of the Communist Parties and progressive forces, and about how to understand and apply principles, has reached a pitch in the councils of our movement that is explained by the enormous broadening of the revolutionary forces and their growing influence on the course of world events. The problems that confront us today are more complex than they have ever been; the situation of our movement has radically changed since the time when the Soviet Union was the only socialist country, blockaded and surrounded by the capitalist powers with a ring of steel.

That simplified all choices. Perhaps this habit of simplification has left us the legacy of a certain mechanical tendency in our thinking, a certain one-sided way of looking at things in which everything was either black or white, a kind of Messianic tendency, an inclination to accept infallibility and an unconditional attitude.

This mental attitude comes into conflict with the new characteristics of the working-class and Communist movement, with the prodigious growth of the revolutionary forces, with the immense number of new problems, new factors, new facts with which we have to reckon when a choice has to be made.

In face of this complexity, the simplest reaction is to express a longing for the old days in which we were "few, but of one mind"; to miss the old monolithic discipline which obliged us to carry out the directives of the leading centre without doubt or question.

But the past does not return. And we need not weep for it. To weep would be tantamount to saying that our future lay behind us, when the truth is that as a Party—like every young creature—we have everything before us. The past was a stage, glorious, tough, dramatic in many instances, but it was an initial stage. If we compare our movement, its youth, with the antiquity of other historical movements, we are just at the beginning. Our forces must be brought together and tightened with an eye to the future, to the future that lies before us.

PROBLEMS STEMMING FROM THE EXISTENCE OF FOURTEEN SOCIALIST STATES

The Communist International was dissolved in 1943 because the growth of the Communist Parties, the different conditions in which they were developing, the diversity of the tasks they were taking up and the need to affirm their national character, made the continuation of a world leading centre and a world-wide discipline out of the question. We approved of the dissolution of the Communist International. At the foot of the document proposing it is the signature of our comrade Dolores Ibárruri. The strengthening of the national character of the Communist Parties at the moment when the war against Hitlerism was at its height meant binding together the defence of class and national positions into one single weapon.

Later, after the end of the war, arose the Information Bureau, made up from various Parties of the socialist States and two large western ones, the French and Italian. This was an initiative in which the rest of the Communist Parties —our own, at any rate—did not participate. The Information Bureau performed, up to a point, the role of an international centre. But the very principle of its constitution was unjust. Seven Parties, however important they may have been, could not lead the communist and workers' movement without its full participation. The reasons which had determined the dissolution of the Communist International remained valid, and plenty of new reasons had arisen which made such a centre even more unsuitable. The experience of the condemnation of Yugoslavia and the subsequent correction of this error put an end to the Cominform in the same way that it had been formed: without the participation of the whole Communist movement.

At bottom, the reason for this second dissolution was not only the incompatibility between a leading centre and the existence of strong national parties. It was determined by the new situation resulting from the defeat of Hitlerism. This situation was mainly distinguished by the formation of new socialist States, by the fact that the Soviet Union, though still the most powerful and decisive, had ceased to be the only socialist country in the world. It is worth asking whether this all-important fact has been sufficiently studied from the political and theoretical points of view in our movement; whether some of the inadequacies and weaknesses of our theoretical work do not stem from that. It was something that radically changed the characteristics of our movement. Perhaps the fact that the socialist States in Europe were founded on the basis of the defeat of Hitlerism

178

by the Soviet Army—combined with the struggle of the national resistance movements and the part played in these by the communists—seemed to make these new problems appear less important. But the subsequent development of each State should have brought them to the fore. Furthermore, other socialist States subsequently arose, such as People's China, North Vietnam and more recently Cuba, which triumphed in different conditions, doubtless favoured by the sharpening of the general crisis of imperialism following the victory over Hitler—also children in a very real sense of the October Revolution, but with a more independent and specific process of development.

Today there are fourteen socialist States at different stages of development. One of them, the U.S.S.R., by the titanic efforts of its people, has transformed itself within 50 years into the second world power and in some respects the first, demonstrating the superiority of the system of collective ownership over that of capitalist private ownership. Another socialist State, Czechoslovakia, came into being already in possession of an advanced economic base. The rest, to a greater or less degree, started from a situation of underdevelopment and have made spectacular progress in a short space of time.

Lenin, in his *State and Revolution*, made a profound study of the role of the State and its significance, showing the need for a State of transition, from capitalism to communism, which could take on many forms but would in essence be *the dictatorship of the proletariat*. But Lenin did not have occasion to study the problems stemming from the co-existence of different socialist States at the same time. The Conference of the 81 Communist Parties touched on these questions cursorily in 1960, stating the general principle that the victory of the working class transcends rivalries among States.

Perhaps, however, this was not enough, and was a too-summary solution of very complex problems. The State, and this includes the State of the dictatorship of the proletariat is, up to a point, a survival from capitalism, from a society divided into classes. That is to say, the need for the State is determined by the task of liquidating capitalism. This explains why the new socialist States may have been hampered by problems inherited from capitalism and even feudalism. One of these, and not a small one, is under-development, a marked difference in the level of economic and cultural development. There are territorial and popula-tion problems. And with them are ideological remnants of the past of each State, which do not disappear of their own accord overnight. Neither must we forget that the constitu-tion of these States has been interfered with, conditioned, by the relation of forces between various world powers at different moments of historical development.

For example, the national tradition of the Polish State was suffused with an anti-Russian, anti-Tsarist spirit, since the Tsarist empire had been the historic oppressor of Poland. Reaction still endeavours, even today, to keep alive these ideological elements inherited from the past, in order to ferment anti-Soviet sentiment in Poland. Without doubt, the Communist Parties in power make great efforts to overcome the heritage of the past, but it is not to be wondered at that as long as imperialism continues to exist in the world these remnants should persist. Or even that, at a given moment in given conditions, they should reappear with considerable virulence.

On top of the problems deriving from historical tradition in the formation of States, others are superimposed. We should not forget that as long as States exist there will also exist, however vestigially, *reasons of State and interests of State.*

In justification for the events of 1956, Comrade Gomulka claimed the need for the alliance with the U.S.S.R. for reasons of State in Poland. The new Polish State, without its alliance with the U.S.S.R., would have found it difficult to keep the recovered territory of Silesia, recovered after centuries of German oppression and domination, from

German imperialism.

As long as States exist, even though they are socialist States, the specific interests of each State will be a real factor, and consequently a basis for the appearance of objective contradictions between States, including socialist ones.

For a long time we have shut our eyes to the existence of objective contradictions in socialism, and in particular to the existence of contradictions between the socialist States. The fact that these contradictions are not antagonistic, that the power of the working class can solve them without clashes, and that in due historical time they can be fully overcome, does not mean that these contradictions are not an objective reality or that they rarely occur. When it comes to planning, for example, the division of labour among the socialist countries, they come out clearly. COMECON is an organisation for collaboration between different socialist States, but at the same time it is a sphere in which some of these contradictions are brought into the open. The sphere of trade relations between socialist and capitalist countries is also propitious for the appearance of these differences. And certainly the actual economic weight of some of the imperialist powers, and the development of the scientific and technical revolution, sometimes provide the imperialists with an instrument for sharpening the contradictions between the socialist States.

These problems cannot be solved by the isolation of the socialist camp, by the erection of insuperable politico-economic frontiers between it and the capitalist world. For this would be radically opposed to the policy of co-existence and of commercial interchange between the two systems, and to the actual need for development of the socialist countries, which cannot disregard the technique or the merchandise of the capitalist countries. Isolation would not favour socialist development; it would make it stagnate.

On the other hand, each Party in power is responsible to its own people for progress and successes in the economic field, as well as for failures. And the people can, at times, make tremendous sacrifices to win or retain a new socialist system. But they need to touch, to see the results of the revolution in the political and moral as well as in the economic field. Socialist governments act under pressure of the wishes and demands of the masses of their countries. It would be idle to deny that this situation may at times be a source of contradictions between one State and another.

Nor is this the only sphere in which contradictions may arise, though in some cases it may be the main one. Sometimes these objective contradictions also involve subjective factors. The way in which the leaders of a State handle contentious problems, if it is not correct, can aggravate them and create serious situations of conflict.

Simple formulas are not enough either to define or solve this situation. The principle that socialist States should be guided by *common interests* is undoubtedly correct. Nevertheless, when it comes to practice, it can be seen that even in the definition of these common interests important differences of interpretation may appear. Though both sides may believe themselves to be actuated by common interests, each can have a different viewpoint. When these differences arise between States, it is not so simple to arrive at a just solution.

The contradictions between States, and even more the subjective handling of them, give rise to more or less *nationalist* attitudes. And neither is it simple to decide the point at which one attitude or another becomes nationalist; the extent to which a nationalism of one kind has been kindled by a nationalism of another kind. Be that as it may, while national States and national problems exist—and they will go on for a long time, since the World Socialist Republic is not yet round the corner—the objective basis for the rise of national attitudes is there. And it is not over-simplified or summary judgments, nor mutual recrimination, which will overcome this factor, but principled, wise, patient and calm handling of the problems.

Life shows us that the vitality of national sentiment is a factor of enormous force which cannot be lightly disregarded. Every internationalist, Marxist-Leninist policy must bear in mind and not underestimate for a single moment the significance of this factor.

Objective contradictions arising from *reasons and interests of State* cause many and various problems inside the socialist camp. This must be admitted as a reality. These are questions on which theory, analysing and drawing conclusions from an experience which is already far from small, has a lot of work to do. It is not enough to enunciate, as we have done hitherto, some all-too-general principles. It is necessary to go deeper. And those who are in the best position to do this are precisely the theorists of the socialist countries. Those of our Parties which have not yet won power approach and feel these problems from the outside, through their effect, for example, on the state of unity in our movements. They affect us, in this way, very directly. But we are not in the best position to tackle them in a definitive way although we feel the need on our own backs, in our own situation, for them to be tackled genuinely and basically. For their consequences also affect us directly.

We should certainly not complain about having these problems, for they are a consequence of the progress and successes of the world revolution, which has already placed the leadership of fourteen States in the hands of Marxist-Leninist parties. They are problems inherent in the growth of the revolution. When instead of fourteen States we have twenty or thirty we shall probably have more problems. Instead of lamenting this we should congratulate ourselves that we have them, so long as we do not shut our eyes to the new questions that our own victories pose for us, so long as we foresee them and watch out for their correct solution by proper methods.

REBUILD UNITY, STARTING FROM THE RECOGNITION OF DIVERSITY

If we are honest, we shall have to admit that the present

situation in our camp, in this respect, is not particularly brilliant. We have achieved an easing of the cold war, a certain easing of tension in the relations between the socialist and imperialist States. This is an undeniable result of the policy of peaceful co-existence. But on the other hand, the place where there is a certain kind of cold war, a state of strong tension, is inside our own camp, among the socialist countries. With fourteen socialist States in existence, it is sad to note that when the *socialist community* is spoken of, it is not what should be formed by these fourteen States that is referred to, but only five of them. It seems as if the *socialist community* were an old sock that goes on inexorably shrinking.

In appearance, the relations between some socialist States are in a state of greater tension than those between them and the imperialist States. For example, it is difficult at times to overcome the disquiet caused by the tension between China and the U.S.S.R. and its possible consequences. Also disquieting is the violence with which polemics are carried on between different socialist countries.

It is neither easy nor pleasant to talk about these problems. But it would be worse to put our heads in the sand and refuse to see them, because only by facing them squarely and tackling them can we put ourselves in a position to solve them.

The glaring division that exists today in the socialist camp and the international Communist movement, exacerbated since August 1968, alarms and in some cases overwhelms not a few Communist Party members, who ask where it is all leading to.

At bottom, both those comrades who condemn the intervention in Czechoslovakia and those who approve it are moved, though for different reasons, by this concern.

Some comrades, even though at heart they realise that it is no solution for today, turn their thoughts nostalgically back to the monolithic unity of the Communist International and are almost ready to think that any stage of the past—

even that of the "cult of the individual"—was better.

The fear that an error or a series of errors on our own part could lead us communists to the fatal result of destroying with our own hands and our own weapons the victories of the world revolution, won in decades of struggle at the cost of so many millions of lives and so many sacrifices; the idea that the present division could even lead to armed conflict between socialist countries—this literally keeps many comrades awake at night.

I believe I am not mistaken in saying that the origin of all the problems that today divide the socialist camp and the world workers' and Communist movement, lies in the moves, the attitudes, of Parties which are in power in their countries. This reveals a factor which cannot be denied : the enormous, decisive part played in our movement by Parties which are in power in their countries. At the same time, it creates a problem : up to what point have *reasons of State, interests of State* decided or at least influenced these moves and attitudes?

On the other hand, while we unwaveringly defend the whole group of socialist States, defend the victories of our camp and extol its successes and achievements—first of all those of the Soviet Union, because of their great scope—can we Communist Parties which have not yet achieved the revolution declare ourselves totally with, adopt unreservedly in all its aspects, the policy of this or that socialist State? Can we declare ourselves completely, without reserve, on problems which we do not know, which we are not having to handle, which are in great measure outside our understanding?

When we are informed in some of the newspapers of the socialist countries that *reasons of State* were a factor in the intervention in Czechoslovakia, can we identify ourselves with this *reason of State*?

We Communists who are struggling in the capitalist countries can reach decisions at a given moment on the basis of the interests of the socialist camp as a whole, a camp

185

which we consider our own. But when a difference arises within this camp and when reasons of State are adduced, it is doubtful whether we ought to reach decisions by this criterion.

Formerly things were simple. There was no other socialist State but the Soviet Union, surrounded by imperialist powers which were feverishly preparing aggression and the strangulation of Soviet power. In that situation, the interests, the reasons of State of the Soviet Union were merged with the interests of the world proletariat. Either the Russian Revolution would continue and triumph over imperialism, or all the possibilities of developing the world revolution would come crashing down, and with them even the reforms won by the working class movement in the capitalist countries. At that time, unconditional defence of the Soviet Union and of each of its decisions was a fundamental necessity. But today, thanks in the first place to the selfsame Soviet Union, the situation has changed. Today—it is not too much to repeat it again—there are fourteen socialist States. When one of them—any one of them—is in conflict with the imperialist camp, there is no problem : our choice is not in doubt. For this reason, despite our divergencies, we are all on the side of Vietnam against US aggression. But when a conflict, of whatever nature, arises between those socialist States, it is not so simple and clear. The old conditioned reflexes of the time when the U.S.S.R. was the only socialist country are not enough now.

We must think deeply about many questions. This is part of the indispensable process of adaptation to today's problems, to the situations and tasks of today. When one thinks of the division in our movement, so recently aggravated; when one feels the pain of this division, it is impossible not to ask, what has gone wrong? what has gone wrong between us?

There is no simple reply, and it must be sought for among all of us. There is a need for a common effort and a very open examination of the problems.

186

The easiest reply would be : what's wrong is that we do not have *a centre, a common discipline.* But if the Communist International was dissolved as a result of the growth of the Communist Parties and the need for them to affirm their national character, then today, when as well as big national Parties there are also a number of States, it is still less possible to direct things from a common centre with a common discipline. This is so manifest that one wonders whether the first thing that is wrong is not a certain inertia whereby the movement tends to be guided—despite solemn discussions and resolutions—by this mentality of *one centre and one discipline.*

The Chinese comrades have tried, and are openly trying, to play this role : to be a world centre and impose a universal discipline. They proclaim it openly. But are they the only ones? Do not other States, large or small, have the same tendency in our movement? But it is plainly evident that proclaimed or not, conscious or not, the pressures for one centre and one discipline divide instead of unite. From the moment when a number try to assume this role, the outcome is inevitable. Practice is conclusive. The pressure towards one centre, one discipline, today automatically engenders polycentrism, which is equally no solution. The existence of one centre or of several centres implies in one way or another the idea of satellite parties. And today, no Communist Party which seriously proposes to make the socialist revolution in its own country and thus fulfil its international duty, can accept the position of a satellite or place itself in the orbit of another Party, however great the prestige and authority of that Party may be.

Each party needs to work out its own revolutionary road, taking account of the concrete situation in its country, applying Marxism-Leninism in a creative way, tackling the new social situation; starting from the present level of struggle and not from the level of that struggle *x* years ago.

The more one ponders about the solution of the problems of our movement, the clearer becomes the need to accept what is becoming a reality today, and in my opinion enriching the revolutionary movement—*diversity*. Any attempt to fit this diversity into a mould, to put it in any sort of straitjacket, to make it uniform would be to act like Canute; there is *diversity* in States and their problems; *diversity* in the socio-historical situations in which each Party is operating; *diversity* in the paths to and forms of socialism.

To shut one's eyes to reality leads nowhere. And diversity exists. The new unity which has to be built, overcoming the present divisions, must start from this fact, take it over, recognise it. This new unity must be built on the basis of much understanding and not a few mutual concessions, above all between the most important parties.

It must be understood that diversity is not a sign of weakness, incoherence or confusion, nor of the abandonment of principle. Diversity is essentially a sign of strength, of development; it is a characteristic of the great strength of our movement and its roots in the life of the people.

Starting from this diversity, we must re-think our entire policy and get to the bottom of what has gone wrong, so as to overcome the division and rebuild unity right throughout our movement.

THE IMPORTANCE OUR ERRORS CAN ACQUIRE

To put the whole of the blame on imperialism for all the difficulties that arise in our camp would be to credit imperialism with a miracle-working power it does not possess. True, imperialism is not a "paper tiger" (and we have never ceased to refute the subjectivist statement that it was one). It still has enormous economic power, a great capacity for manoeuvre, a powerful military force and a reserve of ideologues and politicians, none of which should be underestimated. Imperialism is our implacable enemy. It makes use of espionage, provocation, corruption and intimidation and does not hesitate to adopt the most barbarous methods of aggression, such as for example in

188

Vietnam. It uses open intervention in such countries as Santo Domingo and Guatemala, aggression "by intermediary" as in the Middle East, sabotage and terrorism as in Cuba.

But imperialism is a thousand times more dangerous an enemy when it uses our own errors, the errors of communists, and takes advantage of them to attack and weaken us.

At the time when we Communists were small propaganda groups our errors had little consequence. But when several Parties have become ruling parties in their countries, the errors of Communists can acquire colossal dimensions, and turn into a by no means negligible danger for the cause we represent. An error that starts on a small scale, as Lenin showed, can, if it is persisted in, if it is magnified by self-justification, if it is pushed to its ultimate consequences, become a monstrous one.

The greater the role and weight of a Party, the deeper and more widespread are the consequences, and there is no Party which is free from mistakes. The 20th Congress of the C.P.S.U. was an unforgettable lesson in this respect. To grasp and assimilate this lesson has cost us, and is still costing us, much; to such an extent that there are actually comrades (though they are exceptional) who ask themselves if it was not there that all the ills that now beset us originated. For us it was a real trauma, the denunciation of the faults of one who until then had been for us a kind of demi-god : Stalin. I do not think that everything relating to that period is yet clear—not as regards Stalin's defects, but as regards the causes. What was the origin of all this—the deification of one man, or the unjustified prolongation and crystallisation of methods of power which restricted and even wiped out democracy in the leadership of the Party and the State? At all events, in my judgment, the essential problem posed at the 20th Congress is summed up in this paragraph from the Report of the Central Committee to that Congress :

"The great tasks in building communism require still greater creative effort and initiative by the working people, extensive participation by the masses of the people in governing the state, in all of the vast organisational and economic activity going on in our country. This means that we have to develop Soviet democracy in every way, to eliminate everything that hinders its all-round development." (N. S. Khrushchov, Report of the Central Committee, 20th Congress of the Communist Party of the Soviet Union, February 14, 1956. Soviet News Booklet No. 4, pp. 71-2. Soviet News, London.)

Here, without a doubt, lies the key to all that was new in the 20th Congress. And it is here, too, in this other passage, from the speech of Comrade Suslov on theoretical work :

"Dogmatism and doctrinairism have become widespread, because a section of the economists and philosophers have held aloof from practical life. The essence of the evil disease of doctrinairism is not simply that those infected with it cite quotations all the time, whether they fit in or not; they regard as the supreme criterion of their correctness not practical experience but the pronouncements of authorities on this or that question. They lose the taste for studying real life. Everything is replaced by the culling of quotations and artful manipulation of those quotations. The slightest deviation from a quotation is regarded as a revision of fundamental principles. This activity of the doctrinaires is not merely futile, it is harmful.

"There is no doubt that the cult of the individual has greatly promoted the spread of dogmatism and doctrinairism. Worshippers of the cult of the individual ascribed the development of Marxist theory only to certain personalities and relied entirely on them. As for all the other mortals, allegedly they had to assimilate and popularise what was created by those personalities. The role of the collective thinking of our party and that of fraternal parties in developing revolutionary theory, the role of the collective experience of the masses of the people was thus ignored.

"The party has never tolerated dogmatism, but the struggle against it has become especially acute at the present time. Present-day developments make the task of creatively

190

developing Marxism more pressing than ever. Each day of building communism in our country and building socialism in the people's democracies brings to the fore ever new problems, which should be illuminated by theory. Gigantic changes are taking place all over the world and many problems now appear in a new light. In order to keep in step with life it is imperative to elaborate new problems in a scientific way, further to enrich and develop Marxism. Lenin, in drawing attention to the creative nature of Marxism, stressed that 'we do not regard Marx's theory as something completed and inviolable; on the contrary we are convinced that it has only laid the foundation stone of the science which socialists *must* develop in all directions if they wish to keep pace with life'." (Collected Works, Vol. 4, pp. 211-12.) (Speech by M. A. Suslov at the 20th Congress of the Communist Party of the Soviet Union, February 16, 1956. Soviet News Booklet No. 9, p. 16. Soviet News, London.)

These statements were valid for the whole of our movement. It would be wrong to deny that there has been progress since the 20th Congress. But there are still things that cause disquiet. If one analyses the origin of the counter-revolutionary outbreak in Hungary in 1956, one can see that the reactionary forces and imperialist agents took advantage of the mistakes of the Rakosi leadership which, in the last analysis, were those that had been condemned by the 20th Congress. The events in Poland in 1956, which caused great concern in our movement, had the same origin. And now, twelve years later, the fall of Novotny and the crisis in Czechoslovakia have a similar origin. This is still more alarming : that the same errors are repeated after such a long interval and that action is taken only against the consequences and little or none against the causes. Yet today it is even more important to get to the bottom of the causes of these crises in the development of socialism; more important than to approve or disapprove of the intervention —though not in the least degree underestimating the importance of that, its consequences and the impossibility of keeping silent about it. At bottom, we must get back to the point of departure—the 20th Congress—and carry on with the process that was initiated there.

Yes, we must pay proper attention and attach all due importance to our own mistakes, the mistakes of communists.

There are times when the mistakes of the communists can become our worst and most dangerous enemy, if we do not succeed in courageously rectifying them.

The military strength of the whole socialist camp, from Korea to Vietnam, through China and the U.S.S.R. to Yugoslavia, Albania and Cuba, and its strategic situation, are today so formidable that imperialism could in no wise challenge them. In this whole grouping, the most important and decisive force is undoubtedly the U.S.S.R. But the People's Republic of China—the third great world power—in a few years' time will be, and is to a considerable extent already, a colossal military force. The power of the entire socialist camp, if backed in addition by the struggles of the peoples of the capitalist countries, can safeguard world peace and be a formidable moral and material base for the people's struggle for a new, classless society.

At the same time, the vitality of the ideas of Marxism-Leninism—despite the doctrinaires and dogmatists who regurgitate slogans *ad lib*, despite the efforts of imperialism in the ideological field, and notwithstanding the elements of confusion that may enter the socialist struggle with the arrival of new forces—the effectiveness and power of Communist ideas in present-day society is a plain fact. The year we have just come through has given abundant proof of this.

Certainly, capitalism is still stronger than socialism in the economic sphere. But the progress of the socialist countries is rapidly narrowing this gap, and the struggle of the working class in the capitalist countries can help to counter the advantages of capitalism in this respect.

Imperialism is in open crisis, in open decay. The progress

of the scientific and technical revolution in the most advanced capitalist countries has sharpened the system's internal contradictions.

The total overthrow of capitalism (which must not be conceived in terms of a military victory of the socialist countries over the capitalist countries, but must be seen as a great victory of the working class and progressive forces in the concrete conditions of each country) is today a real and tangible prospect.

This overthrow can be delayed, complicated, even jeopardised, not only by the manoeuvres of imperialism but also by our own faults and mistakes. This is why it is so important to have the courage to analyse and correct them as we go along.

This in no wise implies that we denigrate what has happened up to now, or that we underestimate the successes of socialism, which with all its insufficiencies and faults has built a gigantic launching-base from which we can tackle new, historic, decisive conquests. Neither does it mean that we are picking a quarrel among ourselves. One way or another, the quarrel is already out in the open, and what we are trying to do now is to overcome it. Not by keeping quiet, but by sincerely discussing, as comrades, with no anathemas, no summary condemnations, nor excommunications.

Along the path of class struggle, the victory of the working class, the suppression of classes, we communists pursue the liberation and full development of Man. In bourgeois society this is manifestly impossible to achieve; it is also certain that for some time, above all while the socialist systems remain weak, we shall proceed towards the development and full liberation of Man through a dialectical process which can necessitate some temporary limitation of individual freedoms. This continues to be necessary in certain socialist countries to some extent. But at the same time we must ask ourselves whether some of these rigid structures of the initial periods are not outliving their day, their rigidity having made them not merely unnecessary but counter-productive.

It is thus that something that was positive at one stage can change into its opposite.

One of the most-debated themes among the revolutionary forces today is that of peaceful co-existence between states with different social systems. The policy of co-existence implies that the fundamental contradiction in the world arena between socialism and imperialism must not be resolved by an armed military confrontation, which would jeopardise the very existence of mankind. In our view it does not imply that the socialist states must inflict military defeat on the imperialist states and impose socialism on them. Certainly, as long as imperialism continues to exist there is the danger of a world war, and it is essential that the socialist powers, and above all the most decisive one, the Soviet Union, should be well armed and ready to defend themselves. And we must stress once again, in this respect, the importance to our camp of the existence of so powerful a State of such great weight in the world as the U.S.S.R.

In the strategic perspective of the triumph of the world revolution without war, which is that of the Communist and workers' movement today, the socialist States act as the example of the superiority of socialism over capitalism; as a pole of attraction for the great oppressed masses of the world towards our ideals; as a fundamental moral and material backing for the peoples and the revolutionary forces still struggling against exploitation and aggression.

We revolutionaries who are fighting in the capitalist countries are concerned that the socialist States should develop and be consolidated, and that their example should become ever more clear.

The fundamental role which the socialist States, their policy and their progress, play in the development of our struggle is undeniable.

But the very concept of co-existence also implies that the front line of class struggle and of the struggle against national oppression lies today in those countries where

194

capitalism rules, that the direct combat is waged above all in those countries. This means that the concept of co-existence implies *the need to develop and sharpen the class struggle and the struggle for national liberation in the capitalist countries.*

Each Communist Party which is struggling in a country dominated by capitalism must make the maximum effort to bring together the forces, and undertake the battles, which will bring it nearer to victory. Each Communist Party should be stimulated above all to work out a strategy and develop a line which will increase its authority among the masses and transform it into a powerful class and national force. Each should be judged especially by the ability it shows in this respect.

If we are to avoid an atomic war, if we are to undertake the battle for socialism inside each country, then the importance of the vanguard Parties which today do not possess state power, nor an army nor a state apparatus, but which are struggling effectively to gain power, cannot be under-estimated or disregarded.

Great initiative and creative ability to tackle the specific problems of their countries must be demanded of them; to start from the actual situation in their environment; to grasp what is new, the structural changes that must involve changes in their strategy. It must be demanded that they become the genuine interpreters of the oppressed and dis-contented classes and groups, the genuine interpreters of the national interest.

Only when a revolutionary party is capable of fusing the class interests with those of the nation can it aspire to achieve a triumphant revolution. To pose national interests against class interests has always been a stratagem of the reactionary classes. The great October Socialist Revolution brought together the interests of the working and peasant classes with the general interests of the country, which were demanding an end to the ruinous and destructive war and then the defeat of the foreign interventionist armies and their reactionary bourgeois lackeys inside the country. The Great Patriotic War against Hitlerism, as its name indicates, fused the Soviet people's class interests and their national, state interests into one single cause.

All victorious revolutions have seen national and social factors coincide in certain circumstances.

It is neither realistic nor just to set class interest against genuine national interest. And this goes not only for the socialist but also for the capitalist countries. From this is born the need, as the Communist Parties grow, for them to affirm their national character, their independence. Without a national character, without being rooted in the masses of the people, the proletarian internationalism of a party can lose its real significance and in fact change, whatever the subjective intention, into a kind of cosmopolitanism. Proletarian internationalism acquires all its meaning and effectiveness when the Party that practises it is really rooted in the people.

The accusation of nationalism could be levelled against a Party which adopted an international position that started from the defence of the interests of the oligarchy and imperialism of its country. But a Party which maintains its independent position so as to be able to develop and increase the class struggle and the national struggle against the ruling oligarchy and imperialism, to bring together the necessary forces for the achievement of the revolution in its country is, as Lenin taught us, fulfilling its first international duty.

Today a real Communist Party, nationalist and internationalist at one and the same time, must maintain its own independent character, its own strategy, its own concept of the application of Marxism-Leninism to the conditions of its own country.

It is essential for the Communist Parties of the capitalist countries to have a proper understanding of the policy of co-existence. This necessitates a struggle to prevent a military confrontation between the socialist and the imperialist countries. The best way to achieve this is to speed the defeat of its own capitalism; to develop and sharpen the class struggle in its own country; to approach victory as rapidly as possible. That is to say, international co-existence means the sharpening of the struggle in the countries dominated by capitalism, and in consequence the use of tactics that can isolate the ruling oligarchy and gain the support of the broad masses of the people, of all the forces of progress.

It must be recognised that in some quarters a false concept of co-existence has appeared; that co-existence on the international plane has been interpreted as a reason for watering down the class struggle, for introducing a kind of pragmatic reformism. This error has been intensified by a mechanical glorification and misrepresentation of the possible peaceful ways.

If the front line of the struggle is to be transferred to the countries where imperialism rules, this involves the necessity for special help, and a special understanding towards those parties which are fighting in those conditions. It means that their task must be made easier. If they are small, they must be helped to grow, and if they are large, to become even stronger and more militant; it means that their independence must be respected and furthermore that they must be encouraged to walk on their own feet, without leading strings. This does not exclude criticism or advice, provided this is directed towards helping them to transform themselves into great revolutionary mass parties—national, militant, capable of fulfilling their historic mission.

On the other hand, we have the right to demand that Communist Parties which have triumphed should respect our unity and help us to consolidate and strengthen it. We took a more vigorous part in the polemic with the Chinese comrades when they tried to divide our Party, for this could have undermined its fighting capacity. We cannot permit any attempt against the unity of our Party and the revolutionary forces of our country, sincerely convinced as we are that we are marching along the road that leads to the socialist revolution. This is not to say that we cannot from time to time commit errors of one sort or another; and we will accept friendly criticism to help us correct them wherever it comes from.

Similarly, we cannot accept the tendency for one party or another to assign to itself the monopoly of the true interpretation of Marxism-Leninism. No-one has a monopoly of the truth. In viewing the new problems in the class struggle, those of our Parties which are in the front line possess, for this very reason, an experience which can enable us to make a real contribution tᴏ the development of Marxism-Leninism. This is not to say that we deny the contribution that can be made by the experience of those Parties which have won victory, though the problems they confront may be of a different nature. But in any case, nobody has a monopoly of the definitive truth. Insofar as the question is posed in these terms, the discussion ceases to be theoretical and political and becomes one of dogma; we move into the sphere of religious disputes, a sphere in which excommunication, anathemas and condemnations proliferate; a sphere in which every "orthodoxy" has its heretics, in which neither discussion nor clarification of the truth is possible, only an unconditional toeing of the line or a complete break. All of which is profoundly alien to the scientific character of Marxism-Leninism.

On the other hand, we must declare our principle that peaceful co-existence does not by any means signify respect for the social *status quo* in the world.

When, in connection with the events in Czechoslovakia, we have read in some newspaper or heard from the lips of some comrade the idea that the maintenance of peace entails respect for the present *status quo*, we repudiate this concept, which may reflect one way of understanding reasons of State, but which has nothing to do with a class stand. We do not accept the idea of spheres of influence; we decisively reject it. Precisely because we are operating in the sphere where capitalism rules today, and because we want to smash capitalist rule, we oppose all allocations of spheres of influence and uphold the right of every people to achieve self-determination by all methods, including armed revolutionary struggle if all other possibilities are closed.

For the same reason, we are also in principle against the policy of military blocs, and we fully share the ideas of the Conference of the 81 Parties and the Karlovy Vary Conference in this respect. It is clear to us that so long as NATO exists, the Warsaw Pact (or any other pact which could serve the defence of the socialist countries) is necessary. But we look forward to the overcoming of this situation, for we cannot accept that our countries, by virtue of the machinery of military pacts, should find themselves exposed to the automatic intervention of foreign imperialist Powers if they undertake their social and political liberation.

All the problems of socialism today, complex though they be, are caused by the enormous growth of our strength. Look what is happening in our country : even the Falangists are beginning to call themselves socialists ! Scanning the pages of the Franco press one can find frequent allusions to socialism and its future. No doubt there is something chameleon-like in this sudden change of colour by groups and individuals who are radically anti-socialist. But the chameleon reflects the predominant colour. What these attitudes indicate is the enormous strength that the ideas of socialism are gaining in Spain. This gives us complete certainty that we shall solve our problems. And we shall be victorious. And Spain will be socialist.

ST. MARY'S COLLEGE OF MARYLAND 45383
ST. MARY'S CITY, MARYLAND